Universal Mother

Wishing you the warm embrace of our Universal Mother.
Love, Cecelie

Holly Schapker and Cecelia Dorger

Universal Mother

A Journal for Finding Yourself in Mary

franciscan
media®

Cincinnati, Ohio

Unless otherwise indicated, Scripture texts in this work are taken from the *New American Bible, Revised Edition* © 2010, 1991, 1986, 1970 Confraternity of Christian Doctrine, Washington, D.C. and are used by permission of the copyright owner. All rights reserved. No part of the New American Bible may be reproduced in any form without permission in writing from the copyright owner.

Copyright © 2024, Holly Schapker and Cecelia Dorger.
All rights reserved.

ISBN: 978-1-63253-436-1

Cover and book design by Mark Sullivan and Frank Gutbrod

Published by Franciscan Media
28 W. Liberty St.
Cincinnati, OH 45202
www.FranciscanMedia.org

Printed in the United States of America

"Not all are called to be artists in the specific sense of the term. Yet, as Genesis has it, all men and women are entrusted with the task of creating their own life: in a certain sense, they are to make it a work of art, a masterpiece."

—St. John Paul II

Contents

Foreword by Fr. Johann Roten 1
Introduction 5
How to Use this Book 11
A Simple Guide to *Visio Divina* 13
The Visitation 15
Madonna della Strada 25
Mystical Rose 35
Queen of Divine Grace 45
Our Lady of Częstochowa 55
Queen of All Nations 65
Our Lady of Guadalupe 75
Madonna and Bambino 85
Mother of the World 95
Maryam 105
Seat of Wisdom 115
Weary Travelers 125
The Annunciation 135
A Mother's Kiss 145
Our Lady of the Rose Garden 155
Madonna del Latte 165
Mother of the Incarnate 175
Gate of Heaven 185
Comforter–Mother of Sorrows 195
Pieta 205
Morning Star 215

Foreword

To Be Led

Let yourselves be led into a way of beauty, a way you will discover in a guided meditation of twenty-one portraits of Mary. The meditation will lead to a journal of which you will be the sole author guided by the Spirit.

On this Way of Beauty you will experience surprise and novelty, but also great familiarity with things that come from the heart and speak to the heart. Some of the images will look new to you, maybe even strange. You will have questions. Why do you call this painting Queen of All Nations? Why does the face of Mary look like that of my neighbor next door? Did the Annunciation occur in Africa; I thought it was in Nazareth? And why do these images, all at once, stare back at me questioning, titillating, and moving?

Here is where the Way of Beauty truly begins: When you make room for grace and your own meditation. When the painting speaks to you in image and word. And when the image gives way to daily life, to your own life and experience of the world. When your meditation becomes Visio Divina.

But how can this guided meditation be a Way of Beauty? The Way of Beauty is in fact the way of the Spirit. According to Pope Paul VI the stupendous and mysterious relation between Mary and the Spirit leads to beauty, for Mary is the all-beautiful creature, the mirror without stain, and the supreme ideal of perfection. It is in the Catechism(#721-726) that we find a mini-treatise on the relationship between the Spirit and Mary. She is the masterpiece of the joint mission of Christ and the Spirit; in her the Father has found the dwelling place and temple where Son and Spirit are dwelling among humans, which makes Mary in the eyes of the Church the true seat of wisdom.

Masterpiece

Mary, the masterpiece, is part of the creative manifestation of God's marvelous deeds. Masterpiece of the Spirit's grace, Mary's beauty is a beauty of promise and hope. And so, Mary's beauty is the beauty of beginnings and new beginnings. She embodies a new beginning of God's covenant with humanity, and in her existence, the original and flawless reality of human being is reinstated.

Dwelling Place

Mary is not a masterpiece for herself in splendid isolation. She is a dwelling place for Spirit and Son. She is the bearer of him who is true beauty, the *kallitikos* (Cyril of Alexandria). Ingrained in the very concept of Mary's beauty we find the idea of mission and service. Paradoxically, but not surprisingly, Mary radiates the beauty of the servant or handmaid. Mary does not allow for aesthetic fixation on herself, but points to the *Deus semper major* and to the Church as *semper reformanda*.

Seat of Wisdom

Mary is not wisdom. She is the seat where wisdom is visibly enthroned. Wisdom is the child in the womb, the toddler on her lap, the book in her hand. The role of wisdom is to situate and root human destiny in the ultimate reality of divine origin and finality. Mary, seat of wisdom, is the meeting place between humanity and divinity effected by the Spirit. She is a living embodiment of communion between the human race and God.

The Way of Beauty you are invited to engage in begins and ends in the relation between the Spirit and Mary. Mary is the Spirit's masterpiece, but the Spirit owes Mary his visibility, and where God becomes present and visible, there is beauty. Likewise, it is only in the Spirit that Mary has a face, the face of the *tota pulchra*, but also, and primarily her personal identity. Whatever Mary's face, it would be forever forgotten had it not been modeled by the hand of the Spirit. Where the hand of God touches a human being, there again is beauty.

To Be Led

And so let yourselves be led onto the Way of Beauty created and prepared by Holly and Cecelia. Holly will initiate you to Mary, the masterpiece, to the many different ways in which her portrait has been intuited, meditated on, created and recreated in order to discover the modeling hand of the Spirit. Cecelia will show you the many ways in which the presence of Mary has been and is a dwelling place of beauty and love for heart and mind.

It will be your special grace to discover Mary, seat of wisdom, the one who brings us back to our beginning and ultimate fulfillment in God, our own and most personal way of beauty.

—Father Johann Roten, SM
Scholar in Residence
Marian Library
University of Dayton

Introduction

The Mighty One has done great things for me,
and holy is his name.
His mercy is from age to age
to those who fear him. (Luke 1:49-50)

The Mighty One, the Creator, the Grand Artist enters the studio and places a blank canvas on the easel. God has an idea for healing his relationship with his beloved children. Nothing is as spontaneous as it was "in the beginning," when a mere Word made reality. *This* piece has been in God's heart ever since the gallery of Eden was defaced by sin. Scripture and prophets unveiled incomplete sketches, but now is the hour to bring the painting to life. This masterpiece is the fruit of divine genius. Her name shall be "Mary."

The Virgin Mary was immaculately conceived in accordance with the Artist's plan, which ended with a crown in heaven for her and salvation for her children. No one was more aware that this was a special and unique privilege bestowed upon her than Mary herself. She's humbled by it. In fact, she is the personification of this virtue. Her humility is the starting point in her relationship with each of us. Mary knows of the rough and muddy canvas our lives begin with. She gives us her understanding and compassion. All the while, she reminds us of the truth of God's mercy. Mary wants to join us in our suffering—she doesn't see this as beneath her—and she brings us to the joy of knowing her Son.

With Mary as God's assistant, we receive an outpouring of unmerited grace in abundance. Our true self emerges onto the canvas of our lives. We cannot become the person we want to be on our own—no painting paints itself—but when we choose to walk with Jesus, beauty happens.

Now it is our turn to be placed on the grand easel. In Mary, God shows us a masterpiece, and our Creator can fashion something wonderful from our own imperfect lives. As Genesis reminds us, God can make amazing things out of anything, even dust. We simply need to say yes.

Great saints such as St. Francis of Assisi and St. Ignatius of Loyola have taught me to use my imagination, especially as Ignatius describes in the Spiritual Exercises. The great challenge of the Christian is that we know the story of salvation too well. When we hear the Gospel, our brain automatically takes over and completes the sentences before they reach our ears. Art, on the other hand, shoots arrows of the Word underneath our intellects and pierces our hearts in an ineffable way. Creation continues; newness is born in our spirits. Christian spirituality invites us to imagine what it would be like to know Mary—or even to be her. Art helps us to do that. Creative expression has been used as a heavenly portal for the Catholic church for centuries.

For years, in my quest for Mary, I felt like the Man of La Mancha looking for his elusive Dulcinea. I could never capture her beauty. But this search for Mary is the ultimate Way of beauty, leading to Beauty Incarnate.

The Marian portraits within this book have spoken to many souls. When I give an art tour, I always carry a piece of paper and pencil to record the wisdom shared with me in response to what the viewer experiences. Somehow, a simple image can invite grace. Alone, the image means nothing, but when the heart of the viewer's relationship with God encounters the art, a new window to eternal glory may open.

The paintings in this book portray Mary in various times, cultures, ethnic characters, and styles to show her universal appeal and her love for all God's children. Our Lady is not limited by our constructs. She is forever ancient and forever new, not constrained by history, a flower unwilting and ever fresh. She is Queen of Heaven, yet so ordinary that we can see her in the face of any woman we meet. The great theologians, saints, and artists honor Mary with good reason. She is us!

Michelangelo once chose a piece of marble that had been rejected by the master sculptors for over twenty-five years because it had a significant flaw. That imperfection became the inspiration for one of the world's most admired sculptures, the *David*. The same Spirit that created Michelangelo's *David* is with us now. St. Augustine, in his *Confessions*, likewise described the brilliance and mystery of the Christian life: "In my deepest wound, I saw your glory, and it dazzled me."

I am an artist who makes a lot of mistakes. When corrections are needed, oil painters carefully sand down mistakes on their canvas so that the texture of new paint is not as conspicuous. I don't want thick, arbitrary, and unsightly blobs in the middle of an atmospheric sky. However, in painting this series of Marian works, I have often found that the unintended texture of errors gives an added layer of interest that creates a new and beautiful effect that would not have existed before the mistake. The repetition of applying paint and scraping away the pigment parallels the spiritual life. We sing of this in the Exultet at every Easter Vigil, praising, ironically, the fall of humanity: "O truly necessary sin of Adam.... O happy fault that earned so great, so glorious a Redeemer."

—Holly

Universal Mother is not our first collaboration. Holly and I met through a mutual friend who, knowing that Holly was a painter of the Virgin Mary and I was a researcher and writer about the Virgin Mary, thought we should meet.

We hit it off immediately and loved discussing our favorite subjects: Mary and Marian art. Soon we began doing some work together. We presented talks at exhibit openings of Holly's paintings and thrived on the collaboration. We joined a women's Bible study and consecrated ourselves to Jesus through Mary using the "33 Days to Morning Glory" program. One day, Holly suggested partnering on a book project. But I am getting ahead of myself.

I taught art history as an adjunct professor to college students for many years as I raised my family. A couple of times, a professor position was within my grasp. All my colleagues wrote to the dean in favor of my appointment. "We went with the other guy because your husband is a lawyer," the department chair told me after the review. (My husband is not a lawyer.) Beyond frustrated and feeling powerless, I prayed for discernment. Begged for an answer. "What should I do, Lord? Where do you want me?" I was ready to quit. I was done with the workload and the absurdly low pay. Then my boss approached me and said, "The Art Department wants to team up with Religious Studies for an interdisciplinary course called "Jesus Through the Ages." Will you team-teach it for us?" Jesus. He was the only one I would hang on for. And God knew it. I knew in my core that God had answered my prayers. Sometimes we are given the gift of seeing how God takes our trials and turns them to the good. That class changed everything. The research into sacred art was a joy, absolutely the adrenaline-booster my teaching needed. I would have done it for nothing, and I no longer felt discouraged or underpaid. Teaching about Christian images and their significance to the faithful throughout history was super inspiring.

Not long after teaching that class, I decided to pursue my PhD in art history. After teaching all sorts of art history courses, I knew which areas I did *not* want to study. When I asked myself, "What do I want to look at every day for many years?" the answer was clear: Mary. The most admirable, grace-filled, powerful woman in the world. The art was vast and rich with possibilities.

Images of Mary never failed to move me. A shift in my faith and devotion occurred as I took a deep dive into studying her world. One image in particular caught my attention. I first saw it in the "Jesus Through the Ages" textbook we'd used in class. It was painted by an unknown artist during the late fourteenth or early fifteenth century above a tiny, modest altar in a Franciscan grotto in Greccio, Italy. The grotto is the place where St. Francis arranged the first live nativity pageant on Christmas Eve in 1223 in order to highlight Jesus's humanity. This crude fresco was of a Madonna nursing the Christ child—the Incarnate Son of God, powerless, yet thriving on his human mother's milk. To the left, St. Francis kneels in adoration. It mesmerized me. I wrote my dissertation about the nursing Madonna.

When I saw Holly's works represented here, in all their splendor and diversity, I felt thrilled to contemplate them and write about how they touched me personally. We hope that you, the reader, will connect to the images and stories and find them to be a useful bridge from your lived experience to a closer relationship with Jesus through his mother.

One of my favorite art historians is the deeply insightful Sister Wendy Beckett, a cloistered Carmelite nun who spent seven hours every day in prayer. She wrote, "Great art opens us not just to the truth as an artist sees it, but to our own truth.... You're being invited to enter into a reality of what it means to be human."

Holly and I invite you to enter into your own journey as you meditate on these paintings of Our Blessed Mother.

–Ceil

How to Use this Book

To lose—or find—oneself in these twenty-one Marian paintings, one doesn't need a breadth of knowledge about Our Lady or sacred art. This is a guided meditation journal, with blank spaces for personal, prayerful expression in response to the image, reflections, and Scripture. You might want to consider taking some time with the image of Mary first. Contemplate the painting as she appears before you. Simply looking at art can be an enjoyable experience. However, gazing intently with an open heart allows it to change you. You look at Mary as she looks at you.

We have included a *visio divina* guide on the next page. *Visio divina* is often described as an ancient form of Christian prayer in which we allow our hearts and imaginations to enter into a sacred image, in silence, to see what God might have to say to us.

Next, read and reflect upon the text. Let the Holy Spirit living in Mary guide you. Use your imagination to create notes, reflections, poetry, drawings, scribbles, or scrapbooks with prayer cards, collages, and so on. If you mess up, no worries! You can cover it up and turn it into a scrapbook page. That's the artistic process—let the mistakes lead you to something good. The possibilities are endless.

We invite you to make friends with what happens. The blank space is holding, nurturing, and allowing you to discover who you already are and the beauty within you.

A Simple Guide to Visio Divina

Acknowledge God's loving presence.
Gaze at the image.
Notice what words or emotions enter your heart.
Pray as you are led.

The Visitation

> *The textured circle developed from my painting on top of a previous painting. I didn't recognize it as a good thing at first, but the Spirit reconciled my mistake ... The circle passes through Mary and Elizabeth while representing the deeper reality of God's existence that underlies every instant ... on the surface, however, it simply looks like two cousins excited about pregnancy.*
> —Holly

Holly's Thoughts

The mystery of incarnation bewilders us. We are told that in her perfect humility, Mary was able to accommodate divinity itself and bring it to the world. After she said yes to God, Elizabeth's house was her first destination.

When she heard that Elizabeth was in need, Mary "set out and traveled to the hill country in haste" (Luke 1:39). In the midst of watching this painting develop under my paintbrush, I realized that she will do the same for us. For years, I have struggled with the notion that Mary desires to be with me. How could the perfect Virgin, revered by the angels as Queen of Heaven, want anything to do with my deeply flawed self? I carry a checkered history of addiction, continue to be overly concerned about my own comforts, and have too many attachments to self-centered fears, making mistakes on a daily basis. A question emerged, "If the mother of my Lord should come to me, why would I refuse?" This began my personal journey of conversion to Mary.

The saints say we, too, are pregnant with remarkable possibilities that will manifest with the aid of Our Lady. There are no exceptions. If someone decided to take a drawing class and Leonardo da Vinci came up to their station to offer a couple of drawing tips, would they say no? Mary has mastered the art of the human relationship with all three members of the Trinity and offers us her assistance.

This image is derivative of a detail in an altarpiece. The whole scene is a German tapestry made of wool, silk, and linen, created circa 1410. I chose it as my subject because I wanted to pray with the endearing vignette of the two women affectionately turned toward each other; fruitful designs surrounding them in a festival of joy so overwhelming that even the nascent John the Baptist leapt.

"Within thy wounds, hide me."
—St. Ignatius of Loyola

Mary not only offered help and comfort to Elizabeth, but she also received it. The pears behind Mary are an ancient symbol of femininity because the fruit's shape evokes the woman's womb. Each woman was carrying a child that had an extraordinary role in God's great plan.

The textured circle developed from my painting on top of a previous painting. I didn't recognize it as a good thing at first, but the Spirit reconciled my mistake. God is the giver of love, the receiver of love, and the act of giving love. The circle passes through Mary and Elizabeth while representing the deeper reality of God's existence that underlies every instant. This moment shared is the fulfillment of human need and desire since the Fall; on the surface, however, it simply looks like two cousins excited about pregnancy.

Mary knew the story of Adam and Eve. Did she know that her Son would repair their mistake for all of Israel and for all of humanity? The wooden cross in the middle symbolizes the Passion as Jesus's ultimate sacrifice to save us from sin, in fulfillment of Scripture. He removed the sting of death. Here, our newly conceived Savior is visibly reaching out to John the Baptist as his first welcoming gesture of love. Mary's pregnancy is God reaching out to us.

Cecelia's Thoughts

The excruciating pain of infertility is crushing. Each month, when I realized I wasn't pregnant, the feeling of failure was nearly unbearable. Now, when I'm asked to pray for a young couple's fertility, I remember the devastating disappointment.

Elizabeth must have given up hope, and Mary must have known her pain, shared in it. When Gabriel told Mary of Elizabeth's unfathomable pregnancy, Mary's first action was to visit her. Upon seeing her cousin glowing with life, she utters her longest and most gorgeous speech in Scripture.

The "Magnificat" is a discourse honoring God that echoes down through the ages.

Two women come together to glorify God!

Holly and I have worked together on numerous projects. She had the idea to put our heads, hands, and hearts together for a book to glorify God through Mary. Our work strives to proclaim the greatness of the Lord and, like the symbolism in this painting, we plant a garden redolent with fertile pictures and prayers.

One of the most charming features of images of the Visitation is a depiction of Jesus and John the Baptist in utero. The first sonograms! John was the first to recognize the Savior—even before they were born. Elizabeth felt her son leap for joy when she heard Mary's greeting and, immediately after sensing this somersault, Elizabeth is filled with the Holy Spirit (see Luke 1:41).

In this image of the Visitation, John kneels before his cousin, Jesus. John's reverent posture anticipates his later exclamation, heard in all four Gospels: "One mightier than I is coming after me. I am not worthy to stoop and loosen the thongs of his sandals" (Mark 1:7). John makes clear that Jesus is so exalted that he himself is not fit to do the demeaning work of a slave. This radical language matches Mary's "Magnificat": "He has looked upon his handmaid's lowliness" (Luke 1:48).

The artist places the two holy women in a garden evocative of fertility and creation. Mary and her cousin reach out to embrace each other with familial intimacy as they speak. Elizabeth declares, "Blessed are you who believed..." and Mary redirects the praise to God:

My soul proclaims the greatness of the Lord;
my spirit rejoices in God my savior.
For he has looked upon his handmaid's lowliness;
behold, from now on will all ages call me blessed.
The Mighty One has done great things for me,
and holy is his name.
His mercy is from age to age
to those who fear him.
He has shown might with his arm,
dispersed the arrogant of mind and heart.
He has thrown down the rulers from their thrones
but lifted up the lowly.
The hungry he has filled with good things;
the rich he has sent away empty.
He has helped Israel his servant,
remembering his mercy,
according to his promise to our fathers,
to Abraham and to his descendants forever."
(Luke 1:46–55)

Read the prayer again. While gazing at the image, invite the Holy Spirit to enlighten you.

Imagine yourself saying the words directly from your heart to God's ear.

Write your own discourse praising God for the work he has given you to do.

Madonna della Strada

I emphasized the eyes of Mary and Jesus to be warm and inviting. Their penetrating gaze symbolizes the depth of vision we receive through God's grace. Our inner sight becomes awakened to a state of trusting and believing in God's goodness: we begin to see him hiding in all things, even where we don't expect. —Holly

Holly's Thoughts

Her great, loving care is closer to us than we can possibly imagine. When we honor Mary, we are celebrating the mystery of the Living God and of the perfect disciple. It also reminds us that God wants a similar graced relationship with us.

After a pilgrimage throughout Italy and Spain inspired by St. Ignatius of Loyola, I completed his Spiritual Exercises under the direction of a Jesuit brother. The exercises are meditations and contemplations that ask the seeker to imagine being an active participant in Scripture. This painting is inspired by a fresco that St. Ignatius gazed upon for many hours in the Gesu Church in Rome. "*Madonna della Strada*" means "Our Lady of the Way." It is about the astounding invitation, extended to us all, to be intimate members of the Holy Family. The myriad faces shown in the clothing of the Virgin and Child are people from different centuries and cultures—canonized saints and ordinary people unaware of their holiness. Every one of us is beloved and desired to complete the family.

We receive help each day as we try to walk closer to our Lord. The communion of saints has made it easier for us to find God. Their faces in the garb show their eagerness to assist. There is no greater advocate than Mary. She hears our petitions and presents them to the Great King in her powerful sovereign position as his mother. She imparts her purity to us in order to grow in relationship with Christ. Our Queen Mother reminds us that the One to whom we belong also belongs to us.

We are bonded even more deeply to the family of God than to our earthly family, but everyday family life can help us grow into our true identity. My childhood was a very good one. Hide-and-go-seek was my favorite pastime. Once, my father placed me on top of the refrigerator. It seemed like a long time before he "found" me again. Giggling even now, I see that hide-and-go-seek is a game the children of God often play with their heavenly Father. We try to hide, and we have done so since the very beginning.

We continue the game, even though we cannot truly hide from our patient Father. He knows all our hiding places. Our best delight is in being discovered. He loves this game too. The Almighty One fooled the world by hiding as a helpless baby. His divine genius did this so that we may one day hide under the same protective mantle of our holy Queen along with her Son.

Cecelia's Thoughts

Mother's Day was coming, and I knew just what to get my mom. It was the first year after Dad had passed away, and I knew she would be alone. She had visited us from Florida a few weeks earlier, and one morning, I noticed her pajamas were worn. She loved the cozy, soft cotton of that particular brand. I went to the store that carried them and found her size. I wrapped them up, found a box in which to ship them, took them to my local post office, and mailed them to arrive in plenty of time.

I called on Mother's Day and Mom was delighted with the pajamas. "Oh honey, they're perfect!" she said. With great joy, she went on to tell me about my three siblings' gifts. "I've had the best Mother's Day. An Amazon box arrived, and I knew right away it was from Jim and Jean. It was a book we'd discussed. This morning, I got the prettiest flowers from Joe and Mary, and I am going to dinner with Mary and Bill. I am so blessed! You kids are all so thoughtful." We talked a while longer, then hung up. I found myself scrutinizing the conversation: "How easy is it to click on the Amazon 'Buy Now' button? Or call the florist? And how hard is it to go out for dinner? I am the one who made the effort with my gift." Almost immediately, I realized what a prideful jerk I was. Mom was thrilled with each of her children's demonstrations of love. My small-mindedness taught me a valuable lesson.

> *Blessed are the clean of heart, for they will see God.*
> –Matthew 5:8

Don't we do that with how we love God? Don't we scrutinize other religions or even people in our own faith? We're doing it the right way, and the others are practicing their faith all wrong. They aren't making an effort. But in a flash of divine insight, I realized that God relishes each of our acts of love toward him. God doesn't parse it out, measuring our love by the pound. Like my mom, he's eager for relationship, elated by our loving gestures toward him.

The Virgin Mary's primary role is to bring us closer to Jesus. In this painting, she wraps all of us in her mantle. Each of us brings our own brand of love to her Son. I know she was with me that Mother's Day when I saw myself so clearly, revealing a truth about all of humanity's relationship with God, humbling me and molding me, wrapping me in her mantle of love.

Look closely at the many faces of humanity clamoring to be close to Our Lord. How does God see you?

Reflect on moments when you have judged the actions of others.

What changes can you make in your thinking? Be brutally honest with yourself.

Think about Mary's desire for us to be with God. Mary can be the Queen of our hearts, if only we give her our heart freely.

Mystical Rose

> *When a landscape painter renders a tree reaching for the sun on a bright day, the shadow completes the composition and the colors surrounding it gain brilliancy. To prepare this canvas, I mixed raw umber with ultramarine blue to tone it with the cool, dark colors symbolizing shadow.* —Holly

Holly's Thoughts

Shadows evoke the dark side; however, light shines brighter because of them. I worked on this painting during a time when I felt overcome by my own shadows of past mistakes and was calling on Our Lady to help me forgive myself.

"Mystical Rose" is a title that emphasizes Mary's purity, beauty, and spiritual significance. From ancient times, the rose has been a symbol of mystery. Painting her head adorned with white roses revealed that I, too, am a beloved flower reaching for the sun. We are all cherished, regardless of the shadows we have created. With Mary's help, we encounter transformation. Her sweet fragrance draws us in. The more closely we rely on her, the more we gain a new mind and loving perspective. Even our worst mistakes can become our greatest assets and be used for a higher purpose. Saints have seen value in their flaws because their conversion shows God's unending mercy. They have set the stage for us to meet God's beautiful divine genius in restoring all things.

There is a story of St. Padre Pio in the room of a woman giving birth. Mary appeared to him and told him that the father of the child would die that night. Mary asked Padre Pio to be a spiritual father to the newly born child. "She will be a gem in my crown," she said. When I heard this story, I wondered what sort of crown she might wear. Once, I received a hint. I smelled roses when receiving the Eucharist in Mass without a single flower around. It was Her Majesty's fragrance, which is a common manifestation of her nearness. Perhaps she chose to wear a crown of roses that day, which released the sweet fragrance. May we all spread the same fragrance.

In this painting, our Queen of Heaven appears to us after her coronation, and yet she is ever youthful. Mysteriously, the magnificent flowers in her crown of creation are always fully alive. Her Son came to conquer the mightiest powers of death and so give us life. The cloud in the background produces the mist of his Spirit that descends upon us like the dew. This process takes time, but not one blade of grass or even the tiniest new leaf remains untouched.

> *Your inward life is now sprouting, bringing forth fruit. What a beautiful paradise unfolds within you.*
>
> —*Song of Songs 4:13*
> *(Passion Translation)*

Each rose in her crown represents the blooming of our spiritual lives under Mary's reign. Our "rose among thorns" is always patient. The most honored and fairest person of humanity does not force our spiritual development. She won't cut a single rose within before it has a chance to unfold. Rather, she allows it to slowly bloom in its own perfect time. Eventually, the rewards arise within us.

Cecelia's Thoughts

When I was a little girl, I came home so excited about the May crowning at school that my dad built me a little wooden-stepped shrine that fit into the niche on my bedroom dresser. He sanded it and painted it red, which to this day is still my favorite color. I had been given a small plastic Mary statue in kindergarten, and I put her on the top level of the shrine. The other steps would get small vases of flowers. Lily of the valley, with its tiny bells and delightful fragrance, was my favorite.

That little homemade shrine was a tangible thing that helped root my lifelong devotion to Our Blessed Mother. I still have that modest statue. I have moved it with me to every home, dorm room, single-gal apartment, and finally to the house in which my husband and I raised our family, where it sits on my bathroom counter. Through the years, my children and I would have a May crowning of our own. We'd fashion a small circle of flowers by winding lilies of the valley around a twist-tie and place the crown on a larger statue of Mary. We'd sing classic Marian songs, such as "Bring Flowers of the Rarest."

I have read that Mary loves these rituals and the myriad ways we show our love for her. As you look at this image, notice her pleased expression, her small smile, and her gaze directed intensely at you. The crown of roses is abundant praise, and the reaction from Mary is, "I see you." Magically, the artist has captured Mary's expression of pure love for you, unwavering and true.

Take some time to absorb Mary's love as she looks at you and you look at her.

Think about how you model your love for Mary to your family and friends.

Hold a crowning of your own, and imagine Mary's undivided attention directed at you. Feel her personal, abundant love.

Feel her gratitude as you spread her fragrant graciousness.

Queen of Divine Grace

When I approached this painting, I was struck by Saint Augustine's words: "O Beauty, ever ancient, ever new." I had an image of Mary that evokes something ancient, something from past ages, contrasted with a modern industrial landscape. —Holly

Holly's Thoughts

This painting started as an abstract composition with high contrast. But the paint marks reminded me of a dark and destructive cityscape. This is what humans build if left to their own abilities, absent obedience to God. Think of the Tower of Babel fiasco. My eye travels along the line of smokestacks belching their poisonous vapors, signaling humankind's tendency to remake the world in its own image, an image tarnished by the soot of sin.

What could this have to do with Mary? Well, everything. Mary knows our earthly reality and the desolation that humanity tends to create. She has witnessed the worst. We need only to consider her terrifying existence under the brutal conditions of Roman rule that brought her Son to his savage end. However, Mary chooses to follow her Son's mission.

She appears here as a sorrowful mother, crushed by the sins of the world. Today, she continues her melancholy mission of accompanying sinners on their road to conversion. In our struggles and crosses, Mary is in this world, oppressed by sin. Whatever life situation, whatever cultural situation, Mary is present. She is present to poverty and hardship. She is present to hubris and vanity. Her presence is a suffering presence; her being-with-us is sharing the human condition.

I do not present her only as *deus ex machina*, as the omnipotent fixer, but also as the one who is with us simply as the big sister. She is with us even in this age, the computer age, maybe even without understanding it. It is part of Mary's grace, indeed, to take our place, to wear our shoes.

Our sovereign queen knows our situation in the midst of the mess. She sees our untouchable beauty and holiness when we cannot. The smoke of our sins does not hinder her sight. Mary knows that God can create harmony out of chaos. She defeated darkness with her love during the Passion, and she continues to win again and again as Our Lady of Victory. Christ is the living torch bearing the flames of love that transform the world.

We sometimes fear the wildfire of light within our souls. But those who choose to follow Christ closely become engulfed in the purifying fire of his Spirit. With burning hearts, we are meant to be fearless: igniting every thought, word, action, and situation with God's love, giving glory to his name.

By our Trinitarian baptism, God purifies us of original sin and human messiness. The figure in the smoke is St. Joseph. He had the highest task: protecting and providing for the Christ child and the Mother of God in the darkness of this dangerous world. With their help, we are reminded that even though our lives cannot escape the darkness, it is nothing to be afraid of when we are surrounded by "so great a cloud of witnesses" (see Hebrews 12:1–2). We belong not to Babel, but to the City of God, which has "no need of sun or moon to shine on it, for the glory of God gave it light, and its lamp was the Lamb" (Revelation 21:23).

Cecelia's Thoughts

I am convinced that a whole department in hell is reserved for addiction. A devil sits at a desk, answering the phone: "Department of Addictions. How may we hurt you?" The havoc an alcoholic wreaks on a family has been studied thoroughly by professionals. For me, the unpredictability was the worst part. My father would get sober for a time, and I would feel a huge sense of hope and relief. The minute I saw him pour a drink after a period of sobriety, however, especially after the long dry spells, I would be crushed with disappointment, and the familiar sense of dread would return. I felt like Charlie

Brown running up to kick the football, and every time Lucy snatched it away. But I was just like Charlie Brown, because he hung on to hope from one season to the next. Maybe the Lucy moments exercise our hope muscle, and "hope does not disappoint" (Romans 5:5).

My father was deeply devoted to the Blessed Mother. He and my mom picked December 8, a Marian feast which fell a Wednesday that year, the day of St. Joseph, to get married. They visited Fatima on their honeymoon, and the statue of Our Lady of Fatima that they brought back sat on a shelf in the corner of their bedroom. A painting of Our Lady of Guadalupe graced their wall. My dad taught us the rosary and gathered us to recite it almost every day, a practice I continue still. He spoke about Mary like an old friend, not a far-off entity. One of the last times I spoke with him, I asked him about his devotion to her. His voice was jubilant. "Oh, honey," he said, "I can't wait to meet her." It was as if she were someone he knew online but hadn't met in real life. He *did* meet her a couple of months later, however, when his big heart gave out suddenly. I know she was praying him into heaven at the hour of his death. I am certain she watched over him in his darkest times. His remorse for his alcohol addiction was obvious, undoubtedly due to his active prayer life and deep devotion. Mary was always there for us, bringing us not just peace and love, but fun despite the chaos.

This painting depicts Mary emerging through the disorder of a polluted urban landscape, her face proportionately enormous, serene, and commanding. Dwarfed smokestacks beside her exhale polluted fumes. Debris and lifelessness are implied by the grays and blacks and the sharp edges of abstract shapes. The cacophony of a city's mechanisms swirls around her as she stills the turmoil. This is the powerful Mary of my upbringing. I felt her presence, and I believe she modeled mercy for my dad, celebrating all his beauty, joy, and tremendous capacity for love.

Even though alcoholism no longer affects my life, other sorts of the world's butt-kickings are never far away. Mary's powerful energy is still a constant. She breaks through the clamor of hurt, disappointment, arguments, and sin. She intercedes for us and brings us closer and closer to her Son, Jesus. I marvel. The deeper I fall in love with her, the more I want to live for Jesus, the only begotten Son of God and of Mary.

Look at the painting and contemplate the ways Mary has come through for you.

Write about a circumstance during which you have felt the calming, loving care of Our Blessed Mother.

Our Lady of Częstochowa

I wanted to paint my version of this famous icon because I was struck by the scars on her face. They have become part of the masterpiece, even though they were the result of an act of vandalism. I painted this image on a piece of scrap wood: God can take our sins, even the "adornments" of a vandal, and make something beautiful. —Holly

Holly's Thoughts

Our Lady of Częstochowa, pronounced [CHES] • [STUH] • [KOH] • [VUH], is a venerated icon credited with bestowing many miracles. It resides at the Jasna Góra Monastery in Poland. Each year, Polish Catholics parade the icon through Częstochowa on her feast day, and healings often occur. One year, the Communist authorities ordered that the icon remain indoors. The faithful obeyed, but they found a creative solution. They removed the icon from its frame and paraded the empty frame through the streets. The miracles continued to happen.

My painting is an homage to her dark beauty, which is clothed in mystery. I wanted to contemplate her appearance in this unusual form. She almost looks burned. Theologians teach us that the scar on her face says that "she could not be Mother of Consolation without first being Mother of Sorrows." Mary understands our pain. She also knows our inheritance. Our solution? Centering on God and giving him rightful praise. Spiritually, our wounds become portals for Christ's light to pour into our body and soul. Pain becomes transformed into an asset. Our ability to serve others evolves in a way that would not be accessible, but for the fires we must walk through.

The original portrait was painted on an irregular board made of dark walnut. Mary appears with royal splendor resulting from a heavenly coronation. Her Majesty is not unreachable, to be revered only high on a distant pedestal. She suffers *with* her people in the largest and smallest of battles, whether assisting an army win an impossible victory at Lepanto after the soldiers prayed the rosary or comforting us in our most intimate personal struggles.

I once found myself stuck in the middle of a labyrinth, feeling trapped in failed perfectionism. I realized that no matter how hard I tried, I could never earn God's love. Mary needed to help me receive the mercy of the Father. My hands, wet from tears, were clasped together. There was a silent pause. Miraculously, my left pinky began caressing the back of my right hand. This new soft gesture was Mary consoling me, letting me know that she was standing beside me on my behalf while presenting my prayers to the High King in the cosmic realm. She used my own hands to express her presence. She uses our hands to help others.

As members of the Queen's army, we put on the uniform of kindness and courage in order to be identified among her joyful warriors. "They'll know we are Christians by our love," as the song goes. Imperfect we are. True. But we can still be victorious. As our doting mother, she lends us supernatural outfits from her heavenly wardrobe during the most difficult times—when our hearts are closed from being hurt, when we encounter a difficult personality. She will dress us in the garments of salvation, wrap us in the cloak of integrity, like a bride bedecked with her jewels (see Isaiah 61:10).

St. Augustine defined love as "to will the good of the other." Mary happily accepts our invitation to love the one before us through our eyes, smiles, hands, ears, hugs, energy, and hearts. We gain an alert receptivity within the encounter. Christ happens. Advancing our Queen's undertaking doesn't have to be grand or difficult; as St. Teresa of Kolkata suggests, we can "do small things with great love." These deeds become gems adorning Our Lady and Jesus for an eternity.

Cecelia's Thoughts

Now and then a student will share something shocking and personal. Olivia always called "shotgun" and sat in the front passenger seat of the little bus in which I drove my students on field trips. She'd map our destination on her phone and navigate, preventing us from getting lost. I began to look forward to our conversations. We'd talk about the art we'd seen, her job at Target, her senior thesis paintings, and her mom.

One day she shared that while she was walking along, someone shouted the "N" word at her, spewing ugliness from their car.

It took my breath away. What does that feel like, I wondered. The littering of such vile hatred directed at a fellow human, the human sitting next to me, rendered me speechless. I still rehearse what I should have said to her. No platitude satisfies. That night I cried for her, and I prayed for the beautiful young lady she was, made in the image and likeness of God. Then I prayed for the person (also made in God's image) who spewed the hate.

On one field trip, we went to see an exhibit of Holly Schapker's Marys. On the bus afterward, Olivia said, "I thought at first we'd be seeing all white lady Madonnas. Then we turned that corner, and they started to look like me." I smiled inwardly as I backed out of the parking lot.

In class I told the students about the Virgin Mary appearing as a Native-Latina woman to Juan Diego in Mexico. She even left behind a painting of herself. And in Rwanda, the Virgin Mary appeared as a brown-skinned woman to three young students. She spoke French to Bernadette at Lourdes and was fair-skinned at Medjugorje. Schapker paints the Queen of Heaven and Earth by dipping her brush in a kaleidoscopic palette. Her Marys hail from every corner of the globe.

The Black Madonna of Częstochowa is from the Byzantine icon tradition. Numerous legends surround this icon, and its international reputation was enhanced by Pope John Paul II's three devotional visits and prayers before it. Her dark complexion has been explained as a possible reference to the Song of Songs: "I am black and beautiful . . ." (Song of Songs 1:5). Holly's painting pays homage by echoing the original.

The scratches on Our Lady's cheeks in the icon are the scars inflicted by vandals in the fifteenth century, like a medieval "N" word. Efforts to repair and restore the marks always fail. They reemerge and remain visible to this day. Diving into one's own biases is always a challenging endeavor. I think about my silence after Olivia shared her experience with the bigoted epithet. Did it leave a scar next to the one inflicted by the driver?

Spend some introspective time with this miraculous image. Reflect on a scar imposed upon you as a result of discrimination or bias.

Ask yourself about wounds you may have inflicted by your own unconscious bias. Pray for grace and guidance to leave no more scars.

Queen of All Nations

> **M**ary's face emerged for me superimposed on a modern painting of flowers in a vase. Certain flowers remain in the scene, along with many of the abstract forms behind her. As the painter, I needed to decide what gives life in the composition and what I had to prune away. —Holly

Holly's Thoughts

Art, unlike written language, has no punctuation. Meaning is not confined to a frame. What you see is always the beginning of something else. Here, Mary's face emerged for me superimposed on a modern painting of flowers in a vase. Certain flowers remain in the scene, along with many of the abstract forms behind her. As the painter, I needed to decide what gives life in the composition and what I had to prune away.

Spiritually, I invited Mary to create her own floral arrangement in my heart. Jesus is always pursuing us, especially through Mary, and she does all she can to join us to her Son. I find it takes courage to receive Christ's unearned love. Therefore, I asked Mary to remove anything that prevents me from receiving this love. She opens my heart without any effort needed on my part except to trust in the work and the grace accomplishing it within me. She removes the thorns of my fears, takes out the excess foliage of my character defects, and fills in possibilities for flowering.

In this painting, Mary's eyes reach out. Her face dissolves and disappears, uniting itself with what lies beyond our world: the Kingdom. Mary wants to give us all "kingdom dreams" that transcend our personal talents and limitations so that we rely on God's Spirit. When we accept her invitation, we grow wings, and our souls expand. Assistance arrives like an army of angels marching to our aid. The Queen of Angels sees to it that no matter what obstacles we face, we are never left without Heaven's help.

Our Empress inspires us to rely on Jesus for absolutely everything. "I have the strength for everything through him who empowers me" (Philippians 4:13). We can even ask him to replace our flawed love for Mary with his own perfect love. For it is his divine love that she uses to love us.

I see each day as a painting that can be a new beginning for the Kingdom, and we are the subject matter. What if we looked to the Great Artist who created us and offered God praise and thanksgiving for this masterpiece? It would be strange and wrong for the painted image to fight its creator. But isn't that what we do when we rebel against God in our subtle and not-so-subtle ways? This resistance needs to be pulled out of our hearts like the hard, prickly thorns in Mary's floral arrangements. For me, this painting is about dreams given to us through Mary, dreams of a God who desires that all things be made new and who wants us to realize these dreams. Mary increases the blooming within and beyond us because of her plenitude of grace.

Cecelia's Thoughts

I began volunteering as a jail minister soon after returning from studying abroad for a month in Italy. While pursuing a PhD in art history was wonderful, it was also sometimes crushingly lonely. I said goodbye to my beloved husband and counted off the thirty days, desperately willing the time to pass until he could join me for a vacation. Although I knew no one and could not speak enough Italian to chat up the shop owners, I did encounter the kindness of strangers often enough to give me some measure of companionship. One couple invited me for a cappuccino after Mass. They will never know how meaningful that cup of coffee was to me. It sustained my hunger for community for quite a while. I gathered plenty for my art history research, but I discovered much more about an unspoken poverty of spirit that many endure. The pain of loneliness is excruciating and goes mostly unreported. When I returned home, I asked myself, "How can I relieve people's suffering from loneliness here?"

Then I saw a parish bulletin article about a jail ministry information session. Inmates are certainly separated from their loved ones. I thought I'd go to listen, but I never thought I'd sign up. I felt a sense of peace come over me. No fear or reluctance. "I could do this," I thought.

The first night in the jail, I went to the woman's dorm with Sr. Janet, a pro at this ministry. I will never forget the first inmate I met that night, Lisa. She told me that when she was fourteen, her father put her out to prostitute herself to make money for his addiction. What chance did she have in life? How does someone build a life for themselves after that wretched beginning? I have prayed for Lisa ever since.

When I look at Mary's face in this painting, I am reminded of Lisa. We see Mary's shock, streaks of tears, and promise of love and acceptance—all in one expressive face. Our Lady cries for our hardships even as she smiles her reassurance and affection. She looks unflinchingly at the lonely and suffering Lisa in all of us. She acknowledges our pain but answers it with hope. She is still and peaceful, even as energy electrifies the space around her. Her stillness reflects her steadfast presence, and the energy promises her active role in our prayer life. Take her up on it. She will get it done for you.

What suffering in your life cries out for Mary's gentle guidance?

As you contemplate her love and acceptance, feel her powerful protection surround you.

Feel the energy she breathes into you through the Holy Spirit.

Imagine and write about what Mary affirms as life-giving in your heart and soul.

What would ask her to help you prune away?

Our Lady of Guadalupe

In this portrait, I was surprised to see the shadows take such strong form, casting an unmistakable pattern across her body. It reminded me of Gabriel's promise: "God's Spirit will overshadow you." The sun is behind her, representing the Son, who shines his beautiful light on everyone unconditionally. Mary is turning to the viewer bathed in both the light of Christ and the cool shade of his spirit. —Holly

Holly's Thoughts

My creative process is a spiritual battle, always. There is a dark stage in every project during which I feel lost without a solution. My only hope is relinquishment to God. I sign my paintings with my initials only—to give proper credit to the Holy Spirit. I have come to appreciate this struggle as transitional labor before new birth and to see myself, again and again, as a daughter of the pregnant Virgin.

Juan Diego had a similar experience with Mary's gentle guidance in Mexico in December 1531. Along his path, he saw a beautiful, pregnant woman. Her clothing was adorned with symbols of divine royalty, according to his Aztec culture. She wanted Juan to help her in the divine plan of erecting a basilica in Mexico City to invite a conversion of hearts. It seemed to Juan to be an impossible task. Today, millions of souls have been converted through her influence, and the Basilica of Our Lady of Guadalupe is the most visited Catholic shrine in the world.

In this painting, a sculpture of the Virgin Mary standing outside the Shrine of Our Lady of Guadalupe Church in Santa Fe, New Mexico, comes alive to speak to the viewer—to you. Although without sin, she and her Son still suffered, and they share our pain. Her shadowed face says, "Even though he didn't cause it, Jesus wants your misery. Give *everything* to him and hold nothing back." When we hand over our struggles to him, he breathes on us and we are like statues that come alive.

Mary taught me to never pray anxiously, even in the darkest moments. That would be futile. Rather, we are to thank Jesus for the goodness within our crosses and to look forward to his highest manifestation beyond our current comprehension. He is not limited by this world. In this portrait, I was surprised to see the shadows take such strong form, casting an unmistakable pattern across her body. It reminded me of Gabriel's promise: "God's Spirit will overshadow you." The sun is behind her, representing the Son, who shines his beautiful light on everyone unconditionally. Mary is turning to the viewer bathed in both the light of Christ and the cool shade of his spirit. She is inviting us to join her there. She balances empathetic sadness, acceptance, and perfect joy within her heart.

Mary's queenship is rooted in motherhood. According to the Hebrew tradition, the mother of the king is queen—not the king's spouse. We are all Juan Diegos, with Our Lady inviting us to labor with her in service to her Son, however we can. This gives me great consolation when I am in the studio before a messy canvas and wishing that I had more talent. I may not be Leonardo da Vinci or Fra Angelico, but I can still paint a portrait of the Queen of Heaven, whom I call my mother.

Cecelia's Thoughts

I gave affectionate names to my children when they were babies, as many mothers do. Madeline became "Sugie" because, from the day she was born, she was sweet and sugary. The name "Sugie" appears on my phone when she calls. Ben is "Little Buddy," my cherished pal. Now he is thirty-four and two thousand miles away, but I still call him Little Buddy. My father gave each of his four kids a nickname: Mairsie, Jos, Wheels, and Jazzbo; each tag had its own playful origin. At his funeral, my brother said, "He made us special by the names he gave us."

Our faith embraces naming with great reverence. Certainly, God's name is sacred. The second commandment instructs us not to take the name of the Lord in vain. The Lord's Prayer singles out God's name: "Our Father, who art in Heaven, hallowed be thy name." The sign of the cross uses the name as a pledge to seek God's will: "In the name of the Father." At the empty tomb, Mary Magdalene mistakes the risen Christ for the gardener until he utters her name, "Mary." Imagine how powerful hearing Jesus saying her name must have been.

In the marvelous story of Guadalupe, Mary appears to an uneducated peasant and addresses him familiarly as "Juanito" in his native tongue, *Nahuati*, like a mother speaking fondly to her cherished child. It signals an intimate and dear relationship. Juan is so comfortable with her that he also uses endearments to address the Mother of God.

Schapker uses the icon's most recognizable element, the sun bursting behind her, but she adds the astonishingly personal aspect of Mary turning to address us, her children. "Turn then, most gracious advocate, thine eyes of mercy towards us," we pray.

Open your heart to hear the affectionate name with which she sanctifies you. Be still and listen for it, be comforted by it.

Feel the warmth of her motherly love enfold you as she calls you by that special name.

Imagine Mary turning to you and inviting you to join her in experiencing joy and sadness at the same time.

Have you ever noticed Mary's presence and assistance in a spiritual battle?

Madonna and Bambino

*I*n the original, the artist placed the two figures in front of a black background. I chose to place them in a violet floral setting because Mary did not live in a vacuum but walked in a garden of God's grace. The circular shape reminds us of the Host given to us in Mass. —Holly

Holly's Thoughts

Mary was the woman chosen to be Jesus's mother and then our own. She became his final gift to us before his death on the cross. And we became his final gift to her: "Woman, behold your son." This allows every one of us to claim her as our own, free to express our devotion to her in our various interpretations and greatest accomplishments. Artists through the centuries have taken this claim seriously. It is no wonder she is believed to be the most frequently painted subject in Western civilization!

One secret I've discovered is that when I use my talents to honor Our Blessed Mother, they grow. My life has changed dramatically for the better since I took her into my heart, home, and studio. Resting in her care, like the infant in this image, helps me to experience the world around me with renewed wonder and awe. I can embrace my identity as a child of God. This is not insignificant.

Many of my works pay homage to the masterpieces of great painters. It is my desire to honor these artists, as well as to learn from them. When I first encountered a particular mother and child painting by Pompeo Batoni, I felt compelled to study and contemplate it more deeply. The image of mother and child is a great symbol of the core of the Christian message. God makes himself little (the baby) to make us great (the mother). The love shared between the two figures found in Batoni's work captivated me, as did the composition. I saw a trinitarian triangle formed by the Christ child's right shoulder to his hand; to Mary's left eye; to his right eye; to his shoulder again. I believed this to be an eternal moment captured, a wordless poem inspired by the very mystery of God.

In the original, the artist placed the two figures in front of a black background. I chose to place them in a violet floral setting because Mary did not live in a vacuum but walked in a garden of God's grace. The circular shape reminds us of the Host given to us in Mass. God's *kenosis*, continued in the Eucharist, is a condition for us to reach our true stature as sons and daughters of God, the act and habit being in the divine image and likeness.

> *Amen, I say to you, whoever does not accept the kingdom of God like a child will not enter it.*
>
> —Luke 18:17

I believe grace gives me fear of the Lord just before communion in Mass. With Mary at my side, my heart finds courage to proceed forward. Then, his tenderness enters. My spirit fills with gratitude for the Almighty's transformative nourishment. *Eucharist* means "thanksgiving."

The intimacy portrayed in this image is what we receive in the bread from heaven. It helps us to love her infant Son in everyone we meet, fulfilling Christ's command to love as he loved us.

For myself, this image reminds me that the more I gaze toward Mary, the better I am able to see the beauty within myself. Often, I seem to look into a dirty mirror. I know the reflection is there, but I cannot see it until after I undergo a cleansing process best described as resting in her arms of grace, with her cheek lovingly brushing my forehead.

Cecelia's Thoughts

My husband of forty-one years is not a hugger. He willingly hugs me back, but he initiates few embraces. Over the years, I have learned to delight in the many wonderful ways he says, "I love you," but his way is just not tactile. One night, while he was snoring softly beside me and I was wide awake, worrying about something, I decided to pray. I rolled onto my back to visualize opening my heart to heaven, similar to the way I adjust the rearview mirror before putting the car in gear. I asked Jesus to hold me. Just then, I needed him take me in his arms, even though I didn't expect to feel a physical embrace.

After a while of nothing, I called out for Mary's demonstrative motherly love. I spoke about what was troubling me to both Jesus and Mary.

Restless, I got up to use the bathroom. My light-sleeper hubby muttered, "What's up?" as I passed his side of the bed on my way back. His arm went out, so I moved closer to whisper, "I'm OK." Then his arm encircled my legs and pulled me into bed. I was surprised. Next, he gave me an astonishingly long, intense hug. His strong arms engulfed me, and he held me close, like I'd just been found after being stranded. He kissed my temple and re-hugged me, wrapping me up in a full, hard embrace. Over and over, he squeezed me with unexpected strength and tenderness. He kissed my forehead like you would a child. The warmth of him, the utter surprising depth of his prolonged bear hug, moved me to tear up, unhinged by the unexpectedness of it. I felt so cherished, brought along on a wave of spiritual love manifested in the physical. It had nothing to do with carnality.

Afterward, I curled into the crook of his arm and fell asleep, smiling at the thought that he'd filled a four-decade void. When I awoke in the morning, a richer insight was revealed to me. I marveled that I had been given a supernatural gift. My husband stood in for the eternal embracer from above. It was a glimpse from heaven, a visceral answer to a mentally whispered prayer. This quote came back to me: "The hands of the almighty are so often found at the end of our own arms."

I've researched countless Madonna and Child paintings, but I looked at this one with new eyes after that night. Mary snuggles Jesus tenderly here, kissing his forehead as he hugs her back. Witness the mutual divine love wrapped up in human touch.

Take a moment to ponder parental love from heaven.

Meditate about a way you have felt the gift of heaven meeting earth.

Reflect on a time when the hands of the Almighty were at the end of your own arms—when you became the very image of God while you loved another.

Feel what it is—or would be—like to walk in a garden of God's grace. How might Mary be walking by your side?

Mother of the World

> *An artist is sometimes asked to be an instrument of someone else's creative vision. How do I capture on canvas what is in someone else's imagination? Working together with my patron, we wanted to portray to the students a Mary who is a trusting friend and a protective mother. Mary, who is tangled up in our world, but not bound by it.* —Holly

Holly's Thoughts

In the book of Genesis, we behold God sculpting the first humans. When we create, we are naturally fulfilling our role of being "made in God's image." In our own creativity, we imitate our Creator. This portrait honors the Mother of the One through whom all things were made. She extends her invitation for us to enter her loving embrace, while standing in the foreground between us and the world. She is God's greatest masterpiece. The world is the Artist's gallery. And we are God's works in progress, with Mary as our model.

I was commissioned to create this work to be placed in the chapel at Notre Dame Academy, an all-girls, college-preparatory high school in the Catholic Diocese of Covington, Kentucky. The school is sponsored by the Sisters of Notre Dame of Covington. The school's logo is on the right side of the painting, placed near Mary's heart. The congregational coat of arms of the Sisters of Notre Dame ascends among the fruit and flowers.

In many apparitions, Mary comes to us on our own terms, appearing as one of us. Students at this high school state that they like to come to school with messy hair and chuckle at Mary's own (slightly) tousled bangs dangling on her forehead. Her figure stands in confidence before our crushing culture, as if to say, "The world does not define me. I belong to the Lord." Her open arms guide us to Jesus. His is the radical way by which our hearts find true freedom in this world, without which our lives lack the vibrancy we need. When we live a life "full of grace," the hands of God are shaping us, rather than letting us be eroded and stained by the forces of the world.

The *Theotokos* (Greek for "God-Bearer") has offered Christ her Son to the world and everyone in it. This painting suggests that as we draw closer to Christ, the Artist of our very being is able to more fully realize God's vision in our lives. Mary fosters it, and she facilitates this meeting between us and her Son. Christ in turn draws us into the very mystery of the Trinity, as seen in the dove; into the halo of the Father's glory upon her; and into the face of the Son emanating from the heart that first conceived Him. It is there, in the midst of the Trinity, as though in a studio, that God fashions us more and more into our true image. Then, at last, we, like Our Lady, can become masterpieces fit for the grand galleries of Heaven.

Cecelia's Thoughts

One morning, very early, with my head still on the pillow, I was talking to God. Some of my best prayerful moments happen when my eyes are still closed from slumber and my heart is open, still vulnerable, before full wakefulness has closed its louvered windows one by one. I asked God, "Who are you really? What are you, God? I want to know." As a teacher who has fashioned countless tests, I provided a multiple-choice answer: Are you this? Are you that? Are you the best in Dad? My father was a creative, generous, funny, devoted, loving man. He also had his demons. So, I thought, the best in him, yes. I lay there trying to be quiet, a little embarrassed that I'd once again tried to offer God an answer. Soon, in my heart, in the deepest spaces within me, I heard profoundly, unmistakably, "I am the best in all of you, that's who I AM."

Wow! The best in all of us. I could not have made this up. I am not that smart, not that deeply theological. I was stunned by the great I AM at the end of the statement. I will never forget this grace. I try to remember it when I meet someone wonderful, and more importantly, someone difficult. I search—well, sometimes I search—for the best in the difficult person.

> "Jesus said to them, 'Amen, amen, I say to you, before Abraham came to be, I AM.'"
> —John 8:58

Look closely at the heart of Mary in this painting called *Mother of the World*. See the best in her imposed on her core. There is her Son. Her God. Her Holy Spouse. The best in her.

What questions do you have for God?

Think about the cumulative best in all of us. Oceans of goodness. Mountains of bests. Infinite benevolence.

Think about in whom you must strive to look for the best. Maybe it is someone that you do not like. Or someone who has hurt you. Take time to find God dwelling in that person.

Take time to find the "best in all of us." The divine dwells in all of us.

Maryam

The underlying arabesque patterns behind the figure in the painting represent the diversity of cultures and peoples being woven together as a cloak for Our Lady, who stands at those cultural crossroads bearing God's light. —Holly

Holly's Thoughts

God creates new life in unexpected ways and asks us to look for the divine in all things and in all people. There is no one through whom God cannot reveal something about the Trinity. But it was through Mary that God was first among us, as one of us. In her womb dwelt the Father's desire, written in flesh and blood, "that all be saved" (see 1 Timothy 2:4). God saved Mary first at her Immaculate Conception, that we might later all receive salvation, even if only "at the hour of our death."

I was surprised to learn that Mary has more to say in the Quran than in the Bible. She is revered by Muslims as the greatest woman to have ever lived. She is also celebrated as the mother of Jesus, whom they describe as a "great prophet." The quote around my image is a direct quote from the Quran. "Oh Mary!

Beloved Allah has chosen you, and made you pure, and exalted you above all the women of the worlds" (Quran 3:42).

It gives me hope and great comfort to trust in her desire to untie the knots of conflict, and thus to become the gateway of harmony for Christians, Jews, and Muslims. Her hands never cease working for her children because they are moved by Our Father's divine love and infinite mercy. Our Mother's task is to help us all to be illuminated by the Light of the World, leading us out of the darkness and shadow of sin.

For the Christian, kindness must rule because we have a kind Ruler. The judgments, fake promises, and illusions of this world should be tossed out like bad art not worth preserving. We hand over the ribbon of our lives to Mary for her to loosen and undo the snarl of knots within and among us. She will help us with forgiveness and the ability to love. Then we might better be able to knit bonds of loving kindness between ourselves and our neighbors, even those who are cut from very different cloth.

This painting taught me that our Father's face can be seen in everyone, because Christ's face can be seen, and "whoever has seen [Jesus] has seen the Father" (John 14:9). The underlying arabesque patterns behind the figure in the painting represent the diversity of cultures and peoples being woven together as a cloak for Our Lady, who stands at those cultural crossroads bearing God's light. Jesus came to save every single person and to bring each one to his Father. We are all children of God, and every human being bears God's image and likeness.

Cecelia's Thoughts

Witnessing people's devotion, especially when it's a stolen glimpse, has always moved me deeply. One particular moment changed me. I pulled into a gas station in the middle of the afternoon. A man pulled in at about the same time I did, but instead of stopping near the gas pumps, he steered toward the back, by the dumpster. He got out, unrolled a little rug, knelt down, and then prostrated himself in prayer, fully absorbed and oblivious to his humble surroundings. I watched for a moment, then turned away, not wishing to cheapen the intimate act with my voyeuristic eye.

One of the pillars of the Islamic religion is that the faithful are called to pray five times a day. Muslims are encouraged to develop a direct, personal relationship with the one and only God, the creator of everything in the universe. Our Catholic Apostle's Creed begins with the same belief: "I believe in God, the Father Almighty, creator of heaven and earth." Christians are called to build and nurture a personal relationship with God through prayer also.

After 9/11, I heard lots of harsh, bigoted remarks about Muslims. I was teaching World Art History at the time and decided to combat ignorance with education. During the unit on Islamic art, I booked a tour of a mosque. The docent welcomed us warmly and was eager to answer questions about her faith. There are so many misconceptions, she told me.

"... she will not accept any devotion for herself but will always bring anyone who is devoted to her to her divine Son."

–Fulton Sheen

The young women in my class were to bring a scarf or shawl to wear as a head covering while in the mosque. As we filed in, I was flooded with sweetness when I saw how much they looked like the Virgin Mary. They asked questions about the Islamic faith and about terrorism. Back in the classroom, we studied the Islamic religion. My class of mostly Christian students discovered more similarities than differences.

Holly's painting includes words from the Quran reminding us that God chose Mary and that she is pure and above all women of the worlds. Or, as Elizabeth said in Luke's Gospel, "Blessed are you among women."

After I saw the devout man at the gas station, I became less shy about displaying devotion. When praying while taking a walk, I don't hide my rosary in my pocket anymore. In a restaurant, I begin my meal with the Sign of the Cross and say grace: "In the name of the Father, and of the Son and the Holy Spirit, bless us, O Lord. . . ."

Reflect on how Mary seeks to unite us. Where has she done that in your life?

Has she been the undoer of knots in a relationship? Or in our relationships with others who do not look like us?

Write about a time when you felt a connection that surprised you. How does the example of others' devotion work to change us?

Seat of Wisdom

*T*he white forest background represents her spiritual journey. Mary found her wisdom and voice by pondering in her heart the hills and valleys of her life.... The prominent highlight in her eyes shows a singular focus on Christ's light. —Holly

Holly's Thoughts

Naomi stands 4'9" tall, and she was a bartender in a dangerous neighborhood for fifty years. Enlightened by her experiences, she teaches wisdom in holy simplicity. Her life motto is "Trust God." While she sat as a model for me, Naomi recited Scripture verses pertinent to our conversations. They brought a fresh fragrance to the moment and gave me new perspective. In receiving her trustworthy guidance, I felt as though I was having an encounter with someone who had stepped out of the pages of the Bible.

A painter gains keener eyesight when they paint through observation. We are trained to quiet the left side of the brain that dictates "what to see" in order to simply look at what is before us—what we actually perceive. Without judgment. The right side of the brain, the creative side, perceives lines, shapes, colors, texture, and space. In an interesting composition, these all come together.

During our modeling session, I saw Our Blessed Mother's wisdom personified in Naomi. The white forest background represents her spiritual journey. Mary found her wisdom and voice by pondering in her heart the hills and valleys of her life. All the while, she used Scripture to guide her as a lamp beneath her feet. The prominent highlight in her eyes shows a singular focus on Christ's light. I was reminded of the wonderful advice about the lens by which we see: "The lamp of the body is the eye. If your eye is sound, your whole body will be filled with light; but if your eye is bad, your whole body will be in darkness" (Matthew 6:22–23).

As holy as she was, Mary's life was framed in the same world of hardship that we all endure. The deep red color of the border symbolizes humanity, suffering, and mortality. But by enduring her hardship, she gained wisdom. Mary held closely in her heart the good things that God was doing in her life. Here, Mary wears her signature blue cloak, representing her purity and labeling her as an empress. Traditionally, blue was associated with Byzantine royalty. The woman who glorifies God most perfectly reminds us of the remarkable privilege it is to have the Mighty One inviting us to the same intimate relationship.

Love of God helps us return to innocence. The root of wisdom is humility, which brings a childlike delight in the truth. "Whoever humbles himself like this child is the greatest in the kingdom of heaven" (Matthew 18:4). What does that look like? It looks like the little girl who sees her father and runs to him with exuberance. She joyfully cries, "Daddy!" over and over. Her father is helplessly smitten as he swoops her up into his arms. Both are fully open-hearted. This, for me, is Mary in prayer with the heavenly Father. That's the relationship that Jesus revealed our Father wants with each of us.

Naomi reminded me that God has been trying for this intimacy with us since the creation of Adam. The red floral pattern surrounding Mary also signifies the love, passion, and devotion our Mother passes on to us, along with the luxuriant privilege of owning our inheritance as a beloved child of the Almighty King of eternal glory.

Cecelia's Thoughts

I had to do some banking one busy day, and I jammed the errand between a couple of others. When I got to the teller's window, I gave the young woman a few transactions. She leaned into the task, her long, blonde hair hooked behind her ear, earnest. Then she had to redo something because she made an error. I did not have my arms crossed and my foot tapping, but I might as well have. When she apologized for the delay, I was silent, as ungracious as I could be.

Late that afternoon, I was working on a piece about mercy and decided to look up the definition. Here is the wisdom of the internet search: "mer·cy (mər-sē): compassion or forgiveness shown toward someone whom it is within one's power to punish or harm."

I thought about how I acted toward the teller. As the customer, I had power, and I used it to punish her for her delay. I was ashamed—chastened. I vowed to make amends the next day. I'd make up some banking task, then I'd explain what a busy day I'd had yesterday. That was the plan until I pulled into the lot. I was anxious but resolute. I decided to ditch the excuses and the transaction plan so she would know that I came solely to apologize. That was the truth.

She was at her window. My stomach churned as I stepped up. She greeted me with a warm smile. I said, "I am sure you remember me. I was here yesterday, and I behaved badly to you. I was impatient and rude and there is no excuse for that. I came to say that I am sorry." Now she held the power. And she was unabashedly merciful. "Oh no, you were fine. No need to apologize at all," she said sincerely, immediately forgiving me.

I did not deserve her kindness.

In a prayer meeting, Fr. Bill dispensed this kernel of wisdom: "Justice is getting what we deserve. Mercy is *not* getting what we deserve. Grace is getting what we don't deserve."

When I look at the genius of Mary's expression in this painting, I see a merciful, motherly grin. I feel at any minute her grin will break into a warm, fully open smile. I marvel at Holly Schapker's ability to push the paint around the canvas to arrange such a lively expression, full of mercy.

I received mercy the day I apologized. Why was I anxious before I went into the bank? Because I was worried the teller would treat me with justice. Dish out what I gave her the day before. She did not, and I was deeply thankful, humbled by her benevolence. I imagined and focused on Mary's expression as I drove to the bank, knowing that she would nudge me to a deeper humility by the time I walked in.

Look at the painting and rejoice in the fact that Mary will dispense the Lord's mercy. Her name as Merciful Mother is in prayers, hymns, and litanies. Be assured of it.

Think about a time you were or were not merciful. Reflect about how we can dispense Mary's brand of mercy as we go about our busy lives.

Weary Travelers

> *I wanted to convey the idea of Christ as light, portraying him and his mother in warm light contrasted with a heavy, black background, their radiant love reaching outward. The darkness is the wilderness in our hearts, the Madonna and Child look like a burning bush, asking us to come near.* —Holly

Holly's Thoughts

Mary, born without original sin, may have encountered lovely supernatural moments as she walked the earth. We know from the Gospels, however, that she endured hardship, and that this hardship had a profound purpose. The new Adam and Eve are exiled with the children of the old to lead us back to the Garden. Jesus left heaven to come to where we are in order to bring us back, and to make God's relationship with his children new again.

This painting portrays a snapshot moment of Mary and Jesus traveling to Egypt for safety, escaping the threat of King Herod. Perhaps this is a moment shortly after they received the news of the many slaughtered innocent children in Bethlehem. Did she have survivor's guilt? The infant child didn't come with a handbook. Gabriel announced Christ's birth and then left her in a profound silence. As I painted her face, her expression became perplexed. I felt her identity as a woman who lived in this wilderness. She seems to be carrying a heavy load. Did she ever doubt her parenting skills? Perhaps she *can* relate to our struggles in life about feeling overwhelmed without answers.

She did not float through life. Probably some steps on her journey were heavier than others. God did not spare the Holy Family from the elements. The dark, textured landscape portrays earthly gravity, as well as human sin that wanted to bring her to her knees and hold her back from her mission. Adam and Eve, tempted by the devil, let their trust in their Creator die in their hearts. She could not; neither can we. Eden is not physically available anymore, but we have a new Eve who carried heaven in her arms in the form of a helpless baby. We, too, can depend on the woman God trusted for his divine plan. He *wants* us to walk hand in hand with him again. Wouldn't that be lovely?

I wanted to convey their radiance with a brilliant warm light surrounded by a heavy black color. Their love radiates outward. Again, the deep, dark background is the wilderness space in our hearts, waiting for the flame of God's glory to be the center of our being. The blackness of despair, rage, bitterness, condemnation, and anxiety gives way to peace and joy when we focus our attention on Christ.

Cecelia's Thoughts

Bibi, one of my best friends in my Miami high school, was born in Cuba and was a toddler when she and her family sought asylum in the United States after Fidel Castro's takeover. First, her mom came to look for housing and work because she knew English. She left behind her husband and her two young daughters. Their grandma Lulu brought the two little girls a year later, at ages three and seven, and their dad came the following year.

I learned about immigration before it became a political hot button. I picked up stories at the cafeteria lunch table. I heard about families' desperate attempts to be free from a Communist dictator. But it didn't hit my teenage heart and head the way it did when I had my own three-year-old. That year, my husband had just realized his dream of starting up his own business. Our fledgling business and young family were vulnerable, both unsteady toddlers. We had just built a house. The thought of uprooting dreams and children and moving to another country with no possessions, little money, and a tenuous grip on the culture and language finally sank in.

Bibi's story came back to me. I put myself in her parents' place for the first time. Her father ran a prosperous, family-owned business in Cuba. They had a beachfront vacation home, which would be confiscated by the government, as all privately owned properties were. They carried very little with them. There's a photo taken at the airport of two little girls clutching their dolls, all four of them in matching dresses made by Lulu, their abuela. It was 1961. They were lucky. Many families didn't get out at all. After they were reunited in Miami, the family lived in a modest rented apartment. Bibi's mother made a sign for her husband to carry as he searched for work: "My name is Eddy Diaz. Please give me a job." He was hired as a laborer,

> *Come walk with me as you walked with Adam in your paradise garden. Come taste the fruits of your life in me.*
>
> —Song of Songs 4:16
> (Passion Translation)

painting glutinous, itchy fiberglass on boats. Eddy Diaz's humility moved me to tears. It still does.

The story of the flight into Egypt (see Matthew 2:13–14) is an immigrant's story. The Holy Family fled in the dark of night under the threat from a tyrant who had ordered all boys under the age of two in the Bethlehem region to be massacred. Joseph had been warned in a dream to leave immediately. He and his young family walked over four hundred arduous miles to escape this murderous slaughter. Like Bibi, Jesus was a child, blissfully ignorant of the threat, confident in his parents' ability to keep him safe. The traditional theme of the Holy Family resting on their trek to Egypt is made new in *Weary Travelers*. Notice how vulnerable Mary is, protecting her baby as she puts her trust in her husband's fortitude. Think about how salvation history was fulfilled by their act of humility and love.

What role do we play in this story?

Read the story of the flight into Egypt (Matthew 2:13–14) and think about Jesus, Mary and Joseph as refugees from another time.

Do you have anyone you can ask about their migration story? Maybe it is a relative from a generation or two ago. Put yourself in their place if you can.

The Annunciation

> *The forest of the trees within Mary's white garb represents the complex landscape of human will, from which emerged her fiat. This painting helps us to enter into contemplation, the astonishing "theo drama" of God's great plan. Her story is our story; she was simply the first to live it.* —Holly

Holly's Thoughts

Using visual images along with our imaginations to grow closer to Mary is a successful portal toward holiness that has been used since the days of the earliest apostles. Sacred art and Christian spirituality invite us to imagine what it would be like to know Mary—or even to be her. It is important to remember that when Mary spoke to Gabriel, she was speaking for all of us. Her journey is our journey. As the contemporary patterned background of this image suggests, her remarkable story is still alive and with us today. Because of Mary, every one of us could receive the same instruction as she did from the archangel. "Do not be afraid, for you have found favor with God" (see Luke 1:26–38). In fact, Mary's *fiat*, her "Let it be done," re-echoes whenever we ourselves say yes to God's will.

Nnenna is from the southern part of Nigeria. She was sitting behind me in church. When I turned around to wish her peace, I was struck by her dazzling eyes, beautiful cheekbones, and warm smile. Nervously, I asked her to model for a portrait and, in Marian fashion, she said yes. She was willing to enter into the unknown to serve another.

The suggested tree forest within Mary's white garb represents the unexplored landscape of her answer during the Annunciation. This painting helps us enter into contemplation, the astonishing "theo-drama" of God's great plan. Again, her story is our story; she was simply the first to live it.

Mary offers to share with us her graces, her love, and her mystery, symbolized in the roses adorning her halo. This means she gives us her Son to conceive, bear, nurture, and present. Often, with a little spiritual imagination, we experience the line separating her story from our own to be very thin. St. Paul says we are all members of one body. God's only Son made it that way. For instance, in many Renaissance paintings of the Annunciation, St. Gabriel is kneeling before the humble handmaiden because God commanded the angels to recognize her as his daughter who would become the vessel of his Son. We clumsy humans also share in her experience of having angels kneel before us.

We all imitate Mary and experience her reality every time we attend Mass. When we say Amen to receive the Eucharist, we become vessels carrying Emmanuel, the Son of God. We too, become Christ-bearers, holding divinity and humanity in the temple of our being; we are, by this sacrament, "full of Grace." If they were alive, the Magi might come from afar to pay homage to this "pure, holy, and spotless" gift within us, one that is freely given at a tremendous price. Often, I like to hold the Host on the tip of my tongue as I slowly proceed back to my pew. In the dark church, a feminine presence accompanies me during the early morning hours. A series of angels bow, one by one, as we pass. God has looked with favor on this lowly servant.

Cecelia's Thoughts

My firstborn was due on March 19. Many times, I have reflected on the importance of Madeline's birthday, which finally happened on March 25, the Feast of the Annunciation. I've come to love the feast and its link to that momentous day when my heart was forever changed in two ways. First, no one prepared me for the tremendous unleashing of love that happened when I had her, a cascade of love the size of Niagara Falls that will never dry up. Second, because it was my firstborn's birthday, I believe God wanted to highlight to me the magnitude of the Annunciation and, slowly, I fell more deeply in love with the Blessed Mother.

This week, my daughter and I had an argument. Nobody holds up a mirror, clearly showing you your flawed self, like a beloved adult daughter. Her words ache so much because they're true and I feel gutted to admit it, but the complaints she leveled are those that bugged me the most about my own mom. I'd dearly wanted to fix all the imperfections in this, the next generation; instead, I repeated them.

I wrestled mightily with my part in the quarrel, how I didn't hold my tongue, how I'd damaged us. I went over all manner of speeches in my mind, some decidedly defensive, some *mea culpa*. I prayed for a solution, telling God what I thought should happen. I kept hearing "hand it over to me" in my heart. I struggle with surrendering to God. But I did surrender this situation to him. No speech was delivered.

I recalled a homily from Deacon Joe on the Annunciation:

> God himself became one of us in the womb of the Blessed Virgin Mary. Everything Jesus would later do and teach flows from this event. . . . The Annunciation was God's own design—totally dependent upon Mary's cooperation. When we follow Mary's example of surrendering to God's will, magnificent things happen. Mary gave herself entirely—body, soul, and spirit. Her response is a model for us each day.

I called my precious daughter and apologized. We repaired things. She called me the next day and complimented us for how we managed to heal quickly because our spirits were willing to do so. At Mass the next day, I heard, "the Spirit is alive because of righteousness" (Romans 8:10).

In this painting, Mary receives the angel's message with an attitude of surrender. Her arms are at her sides, indicating that it's all in *God's* hands; she listens to the angel as her eyes focus on heaven, the source of light in the work. She gives her assent. I am reminded of the tremendous fruit borne of surrender.

Meditate on where you need to surrender to God. Think about the marvelous outcome waiting for you if you let God take over. Then let go and get out of the way.

Using your spiritual imagination, consider what it was like for Mary to have been visited by God through the Angel Gabriel.

Use your spiritual imagination to invite Mary to explore a new dream where you say, "Let it be done according to God's will."

A Mother's Kiss

> *The mysterious effect of the painted background developed by accident. An unfinished portrait was leaning against a window. As I entered my studio, light filtered onto the canvas, creating an organic pattern from the leaves of a magnolia tree outside. I was dazzled. Instantly, I began painting what I saw and lost all sense of time. My brush was no longer under my control.* —Holly

Holly's Thoughts

Walking with Mary is choosing to live in mystery. In this painting, Mary kisses a vulnerable and simply clothed infant who is also the King of endless glory. With her, even the simplest moment can be imbued with extravagant grace.

The mysterious effect of the painted background developed by accident. An unfinished portrait was leaning against a window. As I entered my studio, light filtered onto the canvas, creating an organic pattern from the leaves of a magnolia tree outside. I was dazzled. Instantly, I began painting what I saw and lost all sense of time. My brush was no longer under my control.

While painting the reflections of the sunlight, it was as if the forms and shapes liquified—washing down the canvas instead of staining it. This reminded me of the gift of confession that is provided to us through Jesus and Mary. With our permission, our mother gently baths us like children in God's divine mercy.

New birth occurs in the sacrament of Reconciliation. Rather than punishment for our sins, confession rescues us from the snares and traps entangling our spirit, giving relief from the emotional scourging of self-scrutiny. We fall into those traps by straying away like children who run into the street while Mother Mary tries to call us home. She is crying out for her children to return to the safety of her arms. In fact, her whole existence is the return journey home. Serpent Tongue lies and tries to convince us to stay in the wilderness, fending for ourselves as our own gods. But Mary gives us the magical word to return to our true native land. This word is *humility*, for it was *pride* that drove us out of paradise to begin with.

One penance given to me after a confession was to ask Mary to help me to live in a constant state of "Let it be done to me according to Thy word." She shows me how to consistently accept *what is* because I trust in the will of the Father. There is peace in this, the peace of a child who knows that her Father has everything under control. God's will is always more beautiful than my own.

The background alludes to Eden and points to a decision we must make. Do we choose to be the daughter of Mary, the new Eve, living in the kingdom of God, her heavenly realm, or to wander through the wilds as a daughter of Eve? The latter offers only the illusion of the transitory securities of this world. We cling to them like desperate orphans struggling for survival when we could be nourished at the table of heaven.

Eve grasped at the fruit of the tree because she closed her heart to God and didn't trust him. Being faithful to God, Mary embraces God himself: the fruit of her womb. In this, we see God's desire for us all. Our Maker does not merely want to dwell with us in a garden. God wants more. Our Lord wants the closeness and intimacy we see in this painting between Mary and her Son. In the Son, God embraces us, and Mary shows us that our infinite God is astonishingly embraceable.

Cecelia's Thoughts

I was struggling mightily with an affront visited upon me by someone. This person's actions affected my work, and the consequences were palpable. They would impede my progress, and in my own mind, I was convinced that they could halt my progress entirely. I railed against this person—in the shower, in my car, during walks I'd take by myself. The words in my head were ugly. Their nastiness eroded my goodness. As this situation went on, it poisoned my soul and ruined my peace. Then one day, I remembered Jesus's words from Matthew's Gospel: "But I say to you, love your enemies, and pray for those who persecute you" (Matthew 5:44). So I tried it. I would love to tell you I no longer ranted. It is not so. But I said the reluctant prayer, spewed anger, prayed for the foe, growled, prayed—for days, maybe weeks. But I kept returning to the vitriol. Why did I embrace the harsh accusations rather than the prayer for forgiveness? Yet the fury was dimming. These thoughts did not come as readily, nor were they so vehement.

Then one day, I suddenly pictured this image. Mary is kissing this baby. But the baby was not the Christ child in my mind—it was my nemesis. In a flash of insight, a light went on and I understood that Mary loves each child of God with fierce, motherly fervor. I prayed in front of this tender painting, picturing myself imitating Mary. I could feel my anger melt away as I imagined kissing the head of my enemy, forgiving all and finally seeing God's hand in the situation. God's love is so powerful. It was a miracle. I could accomplish this only through the grace of God. It was not my doing. Not at all.

Imagine a love so pure that all injury is pardoned, all insults forgotten.

Meditate on a love so unconditional that, as Mary said to the seers at Medjugorje, "If you knew how much I love you, you would cry for joy." Turn toward that love and accept the grace of God to change you.

Ask Mary to help you see the vulnerability in the one who harmed you. Reflect on them as a child of God.

Imagine sharing a kiss and embrace with your nemesis on the very lap of Our Blessed Mother.

Our Lady of the Rose Garden

I began this piece by wanting to paint a landscape based on a photograph that I took in France. While painting, I realized how boring the composition was. It got stored away. After a trip to Medjugorje, I wanted to paint Our Lady and looked for a suitable canvas. God re-introduced me to my boring friend languishing in storage. —Holly

Holly's Thoughts

The Mother of our church continues to appear to us as a major player in our salvation. Her role didn't end when she was crowned. She comes to us with warnings and yet always leaves us with messages of hope. In fact, she assures us that her Immaculate Heart will triumph. This portrait is derived from a sculpture of Our Lady of Medjugorje. I originally set out to paint seascape until, in my mind's eye, Mary's image appeared on the canvas. The painting can help us imagine the Virgin appearing to us, waiting to engage in conversation. When the young visionaries saw her, they asked her why she is so beautiful; she answered, "Because I love so much."

Revelation 21:2 describes the Church as "a bride adorned for her husband." We can ask the Mother of the bridegroom to prepare us for this event—a request she is always happy to grant. The most beautiful woman in the world is willing to share her beauty advice. Amazing! Rather than a list of products to buy, she points to the ancient secrets the bride of Christ has known for centuries.

She teaches us to apply gratitude to our daily routine. Smiling is becoming. Grumbling is the language of hell; praise and thanksgiving are the language of heaven. Wear the glow of a true conscience, with the most important part of our long-term beauty regimen being going to confession on a regular basis. Sin corrupts the body and decays the weary soul, whereas a purified heart unveils the divine beauty hidden underneath.

Mary's gesture in the portrait is one freely offering her graces, which could fill an ocean. Everything that she has received, she offers to us. Here, she holds rosaries. These prayer beads got their name from the Latin term *rosarium*, which means "rose garden." They remind us of the mysteries of the most beautiful life ever lived: the life of her Son, which Mary helps reveal to us. Praying the rosary is like sitting in Mama's lap and letting her show you a scrapbook of her Son's life. We get to talk to Mary, who is more alive and well than when she lived in Nazareth. She is the world's leading expert on the topics of her Son and living the Christian life. With her help, we come to learn how to love others by learning how her Son first loved us. We inherit our Mother's beauty by coming to know the very source and incarnation of beauty itself.

Cecelia's Thoughts

Twenty-three years ago, I received some difficult news about someone I loved, something awful that they'd done. I was having a really hard time processing it. The day before, I had randomly received a rose from someone involved, but the gift was not connected to the news. "It was just such an unusual color," said the rose giver. A couple of days later, a lady approached me in church with an identical rose and a letter. "I have a message for you from God," she said out of the blue. She handed me an envelope and a light red rose with a brownish-pink edge. I didn't know her well; she was just someone from church.

Here is the letter, including caps, underlining, and bolds:

*You are to know that the path you have chosen in your life is a rose. You have accepted it in totality—the thorns, which are the difficult and/or painful experiences, as well as the beauty of the rose. You have chosen to place your focus on the beauty (the Lord) of the rose, thereby placing your trust in <u>him</u> who is the **<u>SOLUTION</u>** TO EVERY PROBLEM. When you focus on the thorns, you only see the problem and stay at that place. When you focus on the **<u>LORD</u>,** you see the solution to every problem and move on from there in his grace. The growth you experience from each time you focus on him becomes the fragrance of the rose!*

Ceil, he sent you this physical rose as a reminder of the above, as well as to let you know how much he loves you and appreciates your faithfulness and service. He chose the color of the rose, a light red (such as oxygenated blood—his life-giving, active blood) which indicates his living presence in your life. When choosing the red rose for you, I was told not to add baby's breath or ribbon because they would detract from your full attention to the rose (HIM). Sometimes "frills" cloud our vision/priorities.

Please pray to the Holy Spirit for his wisdom and discernment regarding this message.

I was bowled over. Was the message really from God? I prayed to the Holy Spirit for wisdom and discernment and opted to embrace this gift. The news that was so painful to receive was made tolerable. When I shifted my focus to all the good in my loved one, I was able to find God there.

I still have both roses. I hung them on my bathroom mirror light fixture, where they have dried and collected dust. They are a physical reminder of God's sweet grace. The letter and the roses strengthened me. We can find good—find God—in all creatures, all creation. If we look for the thorns, we will find them, but if we take in the fragrance of the rose, we will find God.

In this painting, Mary holds roses out to us. Not a thorn in sight. Her expression is peaceful. She makes herself transparent to keep our focus where it belongs—always on God. There is a tiny cityscape on the horizon to indicate how massive Mary is. She looms over the world, calming us with her peaceful temperament.

Think about searching for God in everyone and in every difficult situation, especially where there is pain. Let's turn to and place our trust in God, as my letter says, "who is the solution to every problem."

Answer Mary's invitation to look past everything else and focus on the beauty of the rose and to "move on from there in his grace."

Write about a problem that needs a shift in your focus. Pray for the grace to find God in it and to rely on God's help.

Madonna del Latte

A good painter never just uses paint straight from the tube. She mixes her colors to give unique depth and vibrancy to her work. Our palette of feelings is similar. We rarely, if ever, experience one emotion at a time, and life is richer for it. —Holly

Holly's Thoughts

The French Impressionists left their studios and painted out of doors to try to capture the effect of light and atmosphere as it was happening. They had to work hastily because the sun is in constant motion; a moment dies as quickly as it comes to be. To the Christian, good news follows the Impressionists' embrace of impermanence.

I was sitting before Rachel as she nursed her baby, and she shared how much her heart cherished every moment with her child. Likewise cherishing the beautiful mystery of the scene before me, I felt an intense desire for the world to stand still. Taking matters into my own hands, I hit the pause button myself with my brush, and watched as a modern Madonna and Child portrait unfolded before me.

With every mark, I tried to capture my model's love, blended with the sadness we all feel in our inability to stop the world from spinning so quickly. Do we not all say that our beloved children grow up too fast? A good painter never just uses paint straight from the tube. She mixes her colors to give unique depth and vibrancy to her work. Our palette of feelings is similar. We rarely, if ever, experience one emotion at a time, and life is richer for it.

It is easy to imagine Mary feeling the same way during her early years with Jesus in this passing world. Simeon's prophecy about her Son during his presentation in the temple— "and you yourself a sword will pierce" (Luke 2:35)—must have articulated a fear she had already considered. Mary treasured and pondered in her heart every experience with her child, and yet she was able to allow them to slip away through her fingers and not weigh her down. She trusted God. She trusted in his goodness and his plan. In the end, the tiny baby in her arms became the Mighty Conqueror of our doom.

> *Where,*
> *O Death, is*
> *your victory?*
> *Where,*
> *O Death, is*
> *your sting?*
> —*1 Corinthians 15:55*

Creation continues. Moments come and go, but God's plan is eternal. One must be in a way awakened to notice the creative process occurring in every moment. Mary is the perfect example of someone who was wide awake in a sleeping world. Once awakened ourselves, we are able to participate in his beautiful mystery with our own loose brush strokes that may seem hasty, but in retrospect, complete God's masterpiece.

Artists often try to paint what cannot be seen. The angels in the background of my portrait symbolize the heavenly realm among us, the eternal immersing itself in our mortal moments. In Mass, we join the angels as they worship Our Father with "right praise." Theologians call the Mass "the perfect icon for heaven." It allows our mortal moment to enter into eternity. We dwell there in the heart of heaven as Our Blessed Mother gazes lovingly upon her children; cherishing us, as we are nourished at Christ's wounded breast.

Cecelia's Thoughts

When I nursed my babies, I was awestruck by two things. God designed an activity that nourishes and nurtures at the same time. My tiny, squishy, vulnerable infants grew fat and substantial on mother's milk alone! The nutrition in my own bodily food is all they needed. Moreover, every time I put my baby to my breast, I fell more deeply in love. It was a love I didn't know was in me. Utter, unconditional, I'd-do-anything-for-you love.

These descriptions are awfully close to God's care for us. He gave us himself as food to nourish us spiritually, and he loves us so intensely and unconditionally that he willfully obliterated our sins by dying for us. He'd do anything for us.

We can analyze the nutrients in breast milk to explain the nourishing physiological aspects of nursing. A hormone, oxytocin, is released in moms' and babies' brains during breastfeeding. It is sometimes called a "cuddle chemical," and it intensifies the bond between mom and baby. Our Creator thought of everything.

In medieval times, the image of Mary nursing adorned the entrances of hospitals and orphanages, to announce the excellent care one could expect from the institution. Medieval people understood immediately that nursing was code for charity and loving care.

In *Madonna del Latte*, this nursing Madonna engages us with her gaze. She says, "See how I love you? I hold you close to my very skin, feeding you as my own. I nurture you and bring you up, so that you can receive the glories of my Son's food and love."

Contemplate how Mary's fierce motherly love feeds us and connects us to Jesus's unconditional love.

Write about a time when you felt fed—nurtured or nourished—either by Jesus or his Mother.

Ask the Queen of Angels to remind you of a time when one of her angels aided you.

Ask your guardian angel to tell you what Mary is like.

Mother of the Incarnate

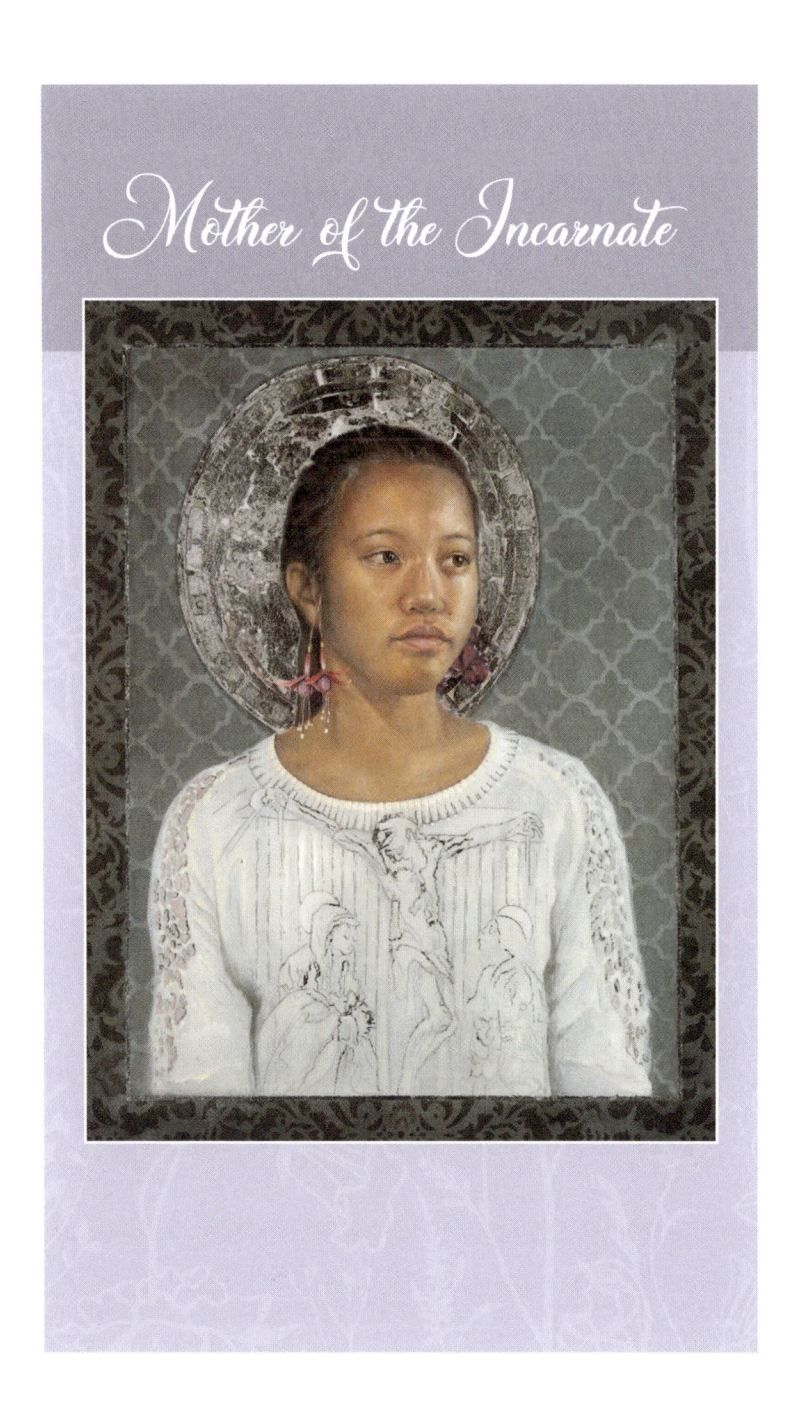

I chose a silver halo to adorn her. The precious metal is associated with divine wisdom, as well as with the moon's soft gleam. Like the moon, whose light reflects the sun, Mary's light reflects the light of her Son, who transfigures souls. —Holly

Holly's Thoughts

The Lord chose her. He chose her before she was born.

Jesus gave himself to Mary from the moment of her consensual response to Gabriel. She received him in her heart before her womb. Just like a mother, she loved everything her Son gave her. I still remember my mom's delighted face when my little hands picked a bouquet of dandelions for her. Imagine Mary's delight when she realizes everything comes from his providence. Jesus *created* the flowers, the trees, the sun, and everything else in the universe—including Mary.

There is a charming legend that the young Jesus playfully hung jewels of ruby and amethyst flowers on his mother's ears. This painting reminds us that the Lord, Creator of life, gives freely without strings attached. Mary is already infinitely beautiful and needs no further adornment. In fact, in order to capture her glowing skin, I delicately painted a series of glazes on her face. Christ continues to pour out manifestations of his love on her. And the Mother of the Incarnate kept every one of them in her heart.

Another "flower" adorns Mary's chest. This one had thorns. There is a subtle tension between the warm and cool coloring in her shirt rather than a colorless white. The cross reminds us of the lengths to which her Son has gone to bestow his warm love upon our cold hearts. She is not wearing this cross as a piece of jewelry. The cross has much to say about who we are and what we stand for.

Everyone carries crosses, even the faces on the glossy magazine covers in the grocery store checkout lanes. We don't know what crosses people are carrying, but Mary knows. I wanted her eyes to remind us to look beyond outward appearances into something deeper. To many in Nazareth, the young mother Mary seemed to live a normal life. And yet, she continuously pondered in her heart the prophecy of Simeon–a premonition and anticipation of Jesus's Passion. The other women around her may have noticed only her beautiful kindness, but the sorrowful mother identity marked Mary's whole life.

I chose a silver halo to adorn her. The precious metal is associated with divine wisdom, as well as with the moon's soft gleam. Like the moon, whose light reflects the sun, Mary's light reflects the Son who transfigures souls. We do the same, even with our flaws and surface craters formed by the impact of our suffering.

Cecelia's Thoughts

Years ago, I was on the board of the contemporary art museum in my city. There were things that went on there that were morally unacceptable. I ignored these occurrences for a while until I couldn't anymore. I prayed for insight. Should I resign? It seemed dramatic. I thought I was cool being on the board. I thought, "I will rotate off in a year or two, and not make a fuss." It nagged at my conscience like a tiny stone in my shoe. One day, I went to Adoration (not a practice in which I engaged often back then). I was asking God for a clear answer. Stay or resign. I finally said, "Could you put the answer on a billboard or in the newspaper or something to make it clear?" I left the church.

I have a little book on the table next to my bed called *Total Surrender*, written by Mother Teresa. I thumb through it and read a page or two from time to time before falling asleep. That night, I read this: "Make the crucifix the center of your life."

The next morning, I opened the paper to the arts section and read a headline: "Andre Serrano to visit Contemporary Arts Center." This is the artist who became famous for his controversial piece called *Piss Christ*, a photograph of a crucifix immersed in a glass of urine. The utter vileness of this piece moved my hesitant heart. I resigned from the board that day. I did not march in, indignant and righteous. I still recall how my voice was shaky and my mouth dry as I told the whole tale to the appropriate board member. I wasn't brave, but I wasn't going to make up some other excuse either. I don't think I had ever acted upon and spoken about my faith so directly before that day. It changed me.

This painting of a young Asian Mary compels us to look closely at her heart. We do not see it at first, because her unique and stunning appearance initially draws our gaze to her face. Once she has our attention though, she directs our interest to the crucifix at the center of her life.

> "Love and sacrifice are closely linked, like the sun and the light. We cannot love without suffering, and we cannot suffer without love."
> — St. Gianna Beretta Molla

When you stray, ask for an outrageous sign to know how to do the right thing. You may be a reluctant disciple, like me, but look closely for the truth.

Imitate Mary, who made the crucifix the center of her life.

Write about a time when you struggled to do the right thing. Why is it so hard?

Reflect on the motives that keep you from total surrender.

Gate of Heaven

To try to capture the complex mystery of Our Lady's intercession, I decided to stencil natural bamboo leaves laid out on the canvas and spray black paint over them. The pattern created a mysterious effect. Then I covered it with a soft white glaze of purification to hold space for this Marian image to appear. I tried to portray the mystery of God's grace at work in our world—through her intercession—in the background with indefinable and enigmatic marks. —Holly

Holly's Thoughts

Mary's act of *kenosis*—self-emptying—elevated her to become the highest creature that ever lived. In this painting, she holds in a holy chalice the world that crucified her Son. Jesus loved the world and died for us, and she shares his vision: she loves this world too. Mary is not a character in her own universe, celebrating her own accomplishments, but rather a helper to the new Adam who is her whole world. But this new Adam did not rise from the dust. He came from above through her, through the Gate of Heaven. She bore the One who would renew the world. And she became the way for people to gain access to God's presence.

Once, a Satanist named Zachary King did horrible things. Inevitably, he became depressed and constantly upset. He also owned a jewelry store. A devout woman walked into his store and saw that the man before her was deeply disturbed. She gave him a Miraculous Medal and explained that it was an image of Mary, the Mother of Jesus. The moment he held it in his hand and saw her, a healing light flooded out the darkness within him. Now a faithful Catholic, he speaks publicly about his conversion.

How did Our Lady intercede for this man? How does she win such favors from our God? It is a mystery. But just as we don't need to understand how a medicine works for us to know that it heals, we know the power of Mary's prayers. When the Gate of Heaven opens, grace floods our lives.

> "For God so loved the world that he gave his only Son..."
> —John 3:16

To try to capture the complex mystery of Our Lady's intercession, I decided to stencil natural bamboo leaves laid out on the surface and spray black paint over them. The pattern created a mysterious effect. Then I covered it with a soft white glaze of purification to hold space for this Marian image to appear. I tried to portray the feeling of her inexplicable grace in the background with indefinable and enigmatic marks. We look to Mary to cultivate in our hearts a mind beyond the one we have now, so that we too can fulfill Christ's mission.

Mary's intercession is powerful and effective in obtaining divine favors and graces for those who ask for her help. I used size and context to portray her transcendental power. The whole world gives way to her influence.

Our most powerful Mother is actively listening to the prayers of her spiritual children in an immanent, intimate way. As I added a layer of warm white to the highlights of her clothing, I remembered Mary's words that started our Savior's ministry: "They have no wine" (see John 2:1–5). As a servant, she simply stated the need to the One who could meet it.

Cecelia's Thoughts

They inch forward one by one, cupping their hands one over the other as they arrive in front of me. Dirty hands fresh from a soccer game, manicured hands, wrinkly hands, shaky hands, big hands, steady hands, and smallish hands. Brown and leathery, pale and pink hands. "The Body of Christ," I say, looking the communicant in the eye each time. Or "The Blood of Christ," and I wipe the chalice's edge and give it a quarter turn. A few open their mouths like baby birds, and I lay the Body of God on their tongues. Distributing the Eucharist is an intimate, humbling, yet also exhilarating act. During the pandemic, only the priest distributed the hosts. The Precious Blood was eliminated. When I could not distribute our Lord, I missed it deeply. It is unifying.

The word *bread* in the Scriptures means that which gives life on all levels. Wine means that which brings joy. St. Augustine's words, "become what you receive" remind us that we who receive the Eucharist take upon ourselves the obligation to become what we celebrate, to become life and joy for others, to become the Body of Christ. Our "Amen" seals that promise and obligation. We receive bread (life) and wine (joy) that have been transformed into the Body and Blood of Christ; we recognize that we are also transformed and live accordingly.

One evening I distributed Communion in the side aisle near the choir. I could hear them singing "Song of the Body of Christ" as I repeated "the Body of Christ" over and over. An exceptional feeling of elation came over me. Utter and unfathomable joy. It is hard to describe. I felt as though I was floating with jubilation, almost out of my body, the Holy Spirit in and around me. I kept distributing the hosts as the choir's percussion matched my beating heart. The song came to an end as the last of the communicants walked off. Slowly, I returned to myself. Later, after I described it, my confidant said, "It sounds like God gave you a glimpse of heaven."

Gate of Heaven is the title of this painting. In it, Mary is a Eucharistic Minister offering Christ to us. The Holy Spirit is with her always, right by her side. Looking at this painting is transformative. Contemplate the mystery of Mary as one who brings God to each of us. As *Theotokos*, or God-Bearer, she carried Jesus and she continues to serve God as she serves him to us.

The Eucharist is where heaven meets earth—God in our hand, God's body taken into our bodies. The Communion line should snake out the door and down the block.

Think and write about how you receive the Eucharist.

Write about your own glimpse of heaven.

Comforter – Mother of Sorrows

> While working on this piece, parts of the ceiling in my studio collapsed. Fallen plaster ripped a hole in the canvas, which I worked into a red, wounded image of the mystical body of Christ. Everyone bears wounds, but none so deep that the Master cannot work them into his art. —Holly

Holly's Thoughts

Mary, Mother of Sorrows, doesn't abandon her children. She entered the indescribable mess of sin during the Passion yet remained victorious in love. Looking to Mary is a way of entering in the holy and triumphant space of our relationship with the One who underwent torture in order to convince us of God's love. It is the world of adoration, mystery, and endurance, with her example reminding us to seek the God of consolation before consolation itself.

While I labored to bring forth this painting, I thought of several things that made my heart ache with sadness: the sorrows of the immigration crisis, the many countries that are at this moment suffering the agonies of war, the victims of brutal violence, the martyrs worldwide suffering for their faith. I imagined an eagle flying above it all, and I thought of St. John's description: "Then I looked again and heard an eagle flying overhead cry out with a loud voice, "Woe, woe, woe, to the inhabitants of the earth" (Revelation 8:13). I remembered a great battle before the *Virgo Potens*—Virgin Most Powerful—conquers the dragon. Our Lady of Sorrows is not crushed by her sorrows but stands victorious in their midst.

Usually, I apply a mixed pigment to the tip of my brush, and then I move the same color around the canvas to create a rhythmic harmony. Everything within the composition is connected, and the whole painting changes with every mark. Without knowing how the artwork will manifest, I try to take the next right action. Eventually, something new is born. The same can be said in this harsh world. A single act of loving kindness, when in union with Christ, can have cosmic effects. If we only do the next right thing, something beautiful always emerges in the midst of this valley of tears.

> *"Capable of great suffering, Mary is a wounded beauty: scarred by life, yet beautiful because she allowed that same pain to transform rather than disfigure her soul."*
>
> —Judith Dupree

Mary's eyes in this painting join Jesus in the Agony of the Garden. He sees every sin of humanity weighing down the wood that he is about to carry, as well as the heartrending, lukewarm indifference of those he loves. She too, will live through every future sinful moment. The barbed wire is a metaphor for the repeated scourgings that separate us from one another and from her. Mary's sorrowful eyes witnessed Christ's carrying of the cross, which was relieved only by death.

While working on this piece, parts of the ceiling in my studio collapsed. Fallen plaster ripped a hole in the canvas, which I worked into a red, wounded image of the mystical body of Christ. Everyone bears wounds, holes in the Master's work. But if this artist can use a little red fabric to heal a torn canvas, imagine what the Son of Our Lady can do for us.

Cecelia's Thoughts

When I was in high school, my older brother Joe asked me if I wanted to chip in on a car for sale for fifty dollars. We called it "Bill and Margie," because before Joe painted it blue with a borrowed spray gun, it was white(ish), with "Bill • Margie" spray-painted across the hood. A car tattoo! Joe did a decent job. Although I remember some rust poking through the wheel wells, I didn't care about that rust. I was just overjoyed to have a car at my disposal—when Joe didn't need it. We lived in Miami, and although we were not on the ocean, we were within walking distance of Biscayne Bay, and we could smell the salt air. I still love that smell and breathe it in deeply whenever we visit, but that rust did not like the salt air, and it slowly inched up the body of the car. In fact, we soon found out that there was rust underneath on the chassis too. Before long, the corrosion caused us problems too expensive to fix.

> *"By his wounds, we are healed."*
> —Isaiah 53:5

I think about that rust when I'm in the line for Confession. How sin takes hold and, if left unchecked, it eats away at our soul, slowly corroding us. We can try to spray-paint over our flaws, but once sin has us in its grip, it creeps in and disintegrates the pure spaces in our soul.

Mary is there for us every step of our rusty journey. She sees us for what we are and loves us through our trials. Like us in all things but sin, she knows suffering firsthand. She wants to safeguard us— if only we let her.

This painting grabs ahold of someplace deep inside me. I find it mesmerizing. The expression on Mary's face is knowing and fully loving, yet sorrowful too, mourning our stubborn inability to surrender to God and to ask for help.

Take your time with this mysterious, multivalent face. Notice the barbed wire, the thorns, a bloody gash on the side. The eagle. What do these suggest for you?

What does Mary's expression say? Let her compassion scour away the corrosive elements in your deepest places.

Repenting is the first step to a renewed self—both the visible outer body and the unseen chassis within.

Pieta

> *My brush gave Mary blue flesh tones, making her face predominantly cool. The blood is leaving her, for a sword has pierced her heart (see Luke 2:35). ... The complementary color to Mary's face is orange, which represents the love of God coming to set the world on fire with mercy through this radical act of self-emptying.* —Holly

Holly's Thoughts

An unexpected palette came about in this painting as I contemplated the moment between Mary and her Son at the foot of the cross. My brush gave Mary blue flesh tones, making her face predominantly cool. The blood is leaving her, for a sword has pierced her heart (see Luke 2:35).

The Great King, the mighty Lion of Judah's tribe, chose to be a victim. For what? Scratching our heads, we ask in prayer what it is that he wants, to which he responds from the cross, "I want you." We struggle to believe that we are worth it, that we are enough. But with hands opened fully wide, Jesus on the cross testifies, "You are worth dying for."

A mother gives birth, protects, nourishes, cares for, teaches, and cherishes her child. It takes supernatural grace to endure the annihilation of her child. Her solid gaze is on him—as always. She was not consumed with self-pity that day in Calvary but rather focused on Christ, offering all her pain to his mission. She teaches us to do the same, joining him in his suffering. The complementary color to Mary's face is orange, which represents the love of God coming to set the world on fire with mercy through this radical act of self-emptying.

This Pieta is a self-portrait; it is also a portrait of each one of us. Mary and Jesus have given everything up for us— and also to us. The rough texture in the painting conveys the pain and messiness of human sin, and the suffering it causes. However, it is in the suffering of Jesus that he draws closest to us, entering into the pain and mess of our lives.

> *By his wounds, [we] have been healed.*
> —1 Peter 2:24

After a profound loss in my life, I heard his gentle voice asking, "Will you stop deflecting my love and finally receive it?" I turned to Mary for help, because receiving him fully is beyond my ability, but was not beyond hers. I gave her my heart and asked to love him with her own love. My hands opened the Bible to a random passage, and my eyes landed on: "I belong to my lover; his yearning is for me" (Song of Songs 7:11). Now, I simply impose the tiny word "my" in front of his name. "My Jesus died on the cross." or "My Jesus made wine from water at the wedding of Cana."

When an artist works intensely on a painting for a long time, she stops seeing it. In order to view her work with a fresh eye, she sometimes flips the painting upside down and stands back to get a new perspective.

In our spiritual life, we often find ourselves in a situation that we impulsively want to reject. Sometimes, we have stories that were created from a troubled perspective; they were "on the easel" too long, so we cannot see what is in front of us anymore. We need God to turn our lives upside down, and often this can happen when he allows some sorrow or suffering to disrupt our reality. What was settled is suddenly up in the air; what was clear is now out of focus. Yet Our Lady teaches us to trust in God even when it makes no sense, even when Christ seems to be lying dead in our arms, for we can trust that we will be resurrected, just as Christ was.

Cecelia's Thoughts

Many of the women I visit in jail are there because of drug abuse. One evening in the prayer circle, we read Mark's account of the poor widow who gave two small coins to the temple treasury. She had contributed all she had. As Jesus pointed out, she gave from her poverty (see Mark 12:41–44). One of the ladies shared a story about the generosity of her friend, Audrey, sitting next to her. A new inmate had been admitted on a night when the dorm was overcrowded. When all the bunks are taken, people are given a plastic "boat" on the floor. It looks like a snow sled. Audrey noticed two things: the new lady was going through an excruciating stage of withdrawal. And her boat had no mattress. Audrey dragged her thin mattress from her own metal bunk, knelt down, cradled the sick lady, and inched the mattress under her. It took me a moment to compose myself before I spoke. I said, "I don't think I know anyone that selfless." The mattress is all the comfort they have in jail, and it is precious little comfort at that. When I hesitate to give something away, I try to remember Audrey's selfless heart.

Mary said yes to being the mother of the Savior and in doing so, she said yes to enormous sacrifices. In this painting, she cradles her only Son after his sacrificial death on the cross. Notice the color of her face. Her pasty pallor expresses a death of her own, a dying to the self. Mary did this out of love for all of us, so that we might be saved, just as Audrey died to her own comfort in a loving act.

Take some time to contemplate what you have had to die to, or still need to let go of, to live more fully in communion with God and with others.

Mary's constant support and assistance will lead us closer to making tough choices. She has your back. Compose a prayer to remind yourself of this.

Contemplate the passion and death of Jesus and embrace the fact that you are worth dying for.

Think about when you've deflected God's love and turn to Mary and give her your heart for help to receive his inexhaustible love.

Morning Star

> *Many portrait artists use a technique mastered by American painter John Singer Sargent that helps make the figure look more alive. We paint loose brush marks around the edges of the canvas, giving contrast to smaller, more precise details in the face. It's the way heavy darkness or pain gives emphasis to the delicate luminosity of joys.* —Holly

Holly's Thoughts

God is entirely too big, ineffable, and incomprehensible for us to understand or grasp. But knowing this, God made himself accessible through Mary. The great mystery need not discourage us. Rather, it invites us into an endless discovery of that which is good, beautiful, and true. Mary is our morning star who lights our journey. We can make her our focus toward holiness. When we lose our way, she shows us where to go and how to live.

Many portrait artists use a painting technique that helps make the figure look more alive. We paint loose brush marks around the edges of the canvas, giving contrast to smaller, more precise details in the face. It's the way heavy darkness or pain gives emphasis to the delicate luminosity of joys.

Mary's mantle is described here more as an energy than a solid fabric. It is used to comfort, inspire, and, of course, to spread love. As her children, we are invited to step into her ever-moving, cosmic mantle of swirling Divinity; to enter the very love of Jesus; to adore our Father; to desire to do God's will. The painting looks unfinished with the rough brush marks. Her story is still incomplete. Our most gracious advocate offers us her faith, her hope, and her love. Every moment that our glances profoundly penetrate each other, we see the invisible God who becomes visible in our neighbor. When our lips join in prayer, and our hearts sing God's praise in unison, we are adding painted strokes to God's masterpiece. The loose marks in the painting direct us to her gaze. This whole painting is focused on her eyes and her vision. We can almost step through them into paradise.

> *May the God of hope fill you with all joy and peace in believing, so that you may abound in hope by the power of the Holy Spirit.*
>
> —Romans 15:13

As I delicately applied the pigment, I contemplated the heavenly realm her most beautiful eyes had seen. She saw the archangel Gabriel addressing her as queen during the Annunciation. My spiritual imagination likes to believe that he returned to her thirty-three years later to announce the resurrection of her Son and to be with her when the risen Christ appeared to her. She saw Jesus ascend into heaven. Mary witnessed the fire of the Holy Spirit pouring out on her children in the upper room. My brush chose to make her eyes green, which is the color of hope and represents the victory of life over death.

Looking forward, Mary knows us and she knows our Lord. She knows the challenges of living in mystery, but she believed what God's messenger told her. She did not succumb to the temptation of confusion and doubt. She is grateful that we received her into our homes and hearts. With her comes her Spouse. God's Spirit always arrives when beloved, invited, and expected. Each of us are called to tell our own story, which becomes our testament. May our feet journey together with her in haste, carrying out her mission of sharing the most beautiful Good News.

Cecelia's Thoughts

I love reading about apparitions of the Virgin Mary. Seers always describe her as exceptionally beautiful, and they note her tenderness and motherly care. There have been thousands of apparitions of the Blessed Mother reported through the centuries. I wonder how many have gone unreported. These appearances of Mary to us earthlings have fascinated me since I saw *The Song of Bernadette* when I was only seven. I remember pretending to be Bernadette. I wanted a visit from Mary. But maybe I have had many visits from Mary, all subtle and most invisible. I say *most* because I have two remarkable stories.

One morning, I was praying the rosary with a friend after Mass. We knelt over to the side where we would not bother the few folks that lingered. As we whispered our prayers, a radiant light started shining in our eyes. We first checked with each other: "Do you see this light?' We checked for a source. No window was in range on that cloudy day, no electric source, no explanation. It was brilliant but not bothersome. Rather, it brought peace. Awed, we continued our prayers as it faded and then disappeared. My thought was that Mary must be happy with these two praying girls. It happened many years ago, and when I ran into my friend the other day, I asked her to tell me what she remembered about the light. We agreed on most of the details. Her wonder was still fresh.

About three years ago, in a different church, I was organizing a presentation of Fr. Michael Gaitley's "33 Days to Morning Glory," a retreat that prepares people for Marian consecration. Another friend was helping me get ready. We encountered a technical snag that morning and decided that a few prayers would be in order. We went to the front of the church and knelt in front of the tabernacle. While praying, a brilliant blue light appeared before us. "Do you see that?" I asked. We looked around for the source. Sometimes the stained-glass windows throw light on the altar, but this cloudy day provided no reflecting colors. My friend snapped a picture of the blue light with her cell phone, and when I look at the picture, shivers go up my spine every time. The technical issue was solved when we got back to work.

Many times, I have checked that same spot in church for the beautiful blue light, looking for a plausible explanation. I have looked on sunny days and cloudy days. I've never seen it again.

I love to ponder these two events.

When I look at this painting, I see Mary's beauty and her motherly love radiating from her like a bright light. Mary looks at me as I look at her. I believe Mary looks at all of us with love all day long and sometimes, just to boost our faith, she shows herself in an act of kindness or in a brilliant light.

Ponder the love that Mary has for you. Notice the small moments of grace she gives you.

Write about a time that you think you may have had a visit from her or been touched by her motherly care.

About the Authors

Holly Schapker is a Catholic oil painter and has been painting for over thirty years. She remains a passionate advocate for the creation of sacred art as an adventure in the spiritual. She has created hundreds of images as prayers to life. Many of her works are on display in Catholic schools, churches, seminaries, convents, and similar institutions. They have been replicated under license worldwide. A graduate of Xavier University, Schapker has spent years in Catholic studies and contemplation. She finds surrender to the Holy Spirit as the true path in the creative process. Holly lives with her attorney husband in Cincinnati.

Cecelia Dorger, PhD, taught art history at Mount St. Joseph University for twenty-eight years. She teaches courses about sacred art at Mount St. Mary's Seminary and School of Theology in Cincinnati, Ohio. She specializes in sacred art, especially images of the Virgin Mary. She is the author of several published articles about the Madonna in art and she has lectured about sacred art nationally and internationally. Lecturing about how sacred art can be used to facilitate prayer is a favorite pursuit. Dorger lives in Kentucky with her husband; they have two married children and three grandchildren.